Richard Garnett, Percy Bysshe Shelley

Poems selected from Percy Bysshe Shelley

Richard Garnett, Percy Bysshe Shelley

Poems selected from Percy Bysshe Shelley

ISBN/EAN: 9783744712415

Printed in Europe, USA, Canada, Australia, Japan

Cover: Foto ©Thomas Meinert / pixelio.de

More available books at **www.hansebooks.com**

PERCY BYSSHE SHELLEY

W E Heitland
St John's College
Cambridge
Feb 1880.

SHELLEY'S MINOR POEMS.

Percy Bysshe Shelley.

Cor Cordium.

Natus IV Aug. MDCCXCII

Obiit VIII Jul. MDCCCXXII

"*Nothing of him that doth fade,
But doth suffer a sea change
Into something rich and strange.*"

POEMS

SELECTED FROM

PERCY BYSSHE SHELLEY

WITH PREFACE BY

RICHARD GARNETT

LONDON
C. KEGAN PAUL & CO., 1, PATERNOSTER SQUARE

MDCCCLXXX

CONTENTS.

EARLY.

	PAGE
ALASTOR; OR, THE SPIRIT OF SOLITUDE	1
TO COLERIDGE	30
STANZAS. ["Away! the moor is dark."]	32
MUTABILITY	34
"THERE IS NO WORK," etc.	35
A SUMMER-EVENING CHURCH-YARD	36
TO WORDSWORTH	38
THE DÆMON OF THE WORLD	39
TO MARY WOLLSTONECRAFT GODWIN	65
LINES. ["The cold earth slept below."]	67
TO ———. ["Yet look on me."]	68

1816.

MONT BLANC	69
ON FANNY GODWIN	75
HYMN TO INTELLECTUAL BEAUTY	76
THE SUNSET	80
MARIANNE'S DREAM	82
TO CONSTANTIA, SINGING	90
TO CONSTANTIA	92

CONTENTS.

1817.

	PAGE
SONNET. OZYMANDIAS	93
LINES. ["That time is dead for ever, child."]	94
DEATH	95
TO WILLIAM SHELLEY	96
LINES TO A CRITIC	98

1818.

TO MARY	99
SONNET. ["Lift not the painted veil."]	100
LINES WRITTEN AMONG THE EUGANEAN HILLS	101
JULIAN AND MADDALO	116
SONG, ON A FADED VIOLET	141
STANZAS WRITTEN IN DEJECTION NEAR NAPLES	142
THE PAST	144
PASSAGE OF THE APENNINES	145
INVOCATION TO MISERY	145
SONG FOR "TASSO"	149

1819.

ODE TO HEAVEN	150
AN EXHORTATION	152
ODE TO THE WEST WIND	154
ODE TO THE ASSERTORS OF LIBERTY	158
THE INDIAN SERENADE	160
TO SOPHIA	161
ON THE MEDUSA	163
TO WILLIAM SHELLEY	165

1820.

THE SENSITIVE PLANT	166
THE CLOUD	180
TO A SKYLARK	184

CONTENTS.

	PAGE
ODE TO LIBERTY	189
EPIPSYCHIDION	202
DEATH	226
AUTUMN	227
LETTER TO MARIA GISBORNE	228
THE WITCH OF ATLAS	241
THE WANING MOON	272
TO THE MOON	272
LOVE'S PHILOSOPHY	273
ARETHUSA	274
THE QUESTION	278
GOOD NIGHT	280
HYMN OF APOLLO	281
HYMN OF PAN	283
THE TWO SPIRITS	285
TO ———. ["I fear thy kisses, gentle maiden."]	287
SONG OF PROSERPINE	288
SUMMER AND WINTER	289
ODE TO NAPLES	290
LIBERTY	297
THE WORLD'S WANDERERS	299
AN ALLEGORY	300
TIME LONG PAST	301
SONNET. ["Ye hasten to the dead."]	302
LINES TO A REVIEWER	303

1821.

ON KEATS	303
ADONAIS	304
ON THE DEATH OF NAPOLEON	328
DIRGE FOR THE YEAR	330
TO NIGHT	331
TO EMILIA VIVIANI	333

CONTENTS.

	PAGE
TIME	333
CHORUS FROM HELLAS	334
LINES. ["Far, far away."]	335
THE FUGITIVES	336
SONG. ["Rarely, rarely comest thou."]	339
TO ———. ["Music, when soft voices die."]	341
MUTABILITY	342
SONNET. POLITICAL GREATNESS	343
THE AZIOLA	344
REMEMBRANCE	345
A LAMENT	346
TO EDWARD WILLIAMS	347
TO ———. ["One word is too often profaned."]	350
TO ———. ["When passion's trance."]	351
A BRIDAL SONG	352
GINEVRA	353
EVENING	362
TO-MORROW	363
MUSIC	364

1822.

THE ZUCCA	365
A DIRGE	369
THE MAGNETIC LADY TO HER PATIENT	370
LINES. ["When the lamp is shattered."]	372
TO JANE — THE INVITATION	374
TO JANE — THE RECOLLECTION	377
WITH A GUITAR, TO JANE	381
TO JANE	384
LINES WRITTEN IN THE BAY OF LERICI	386
LINES. ["We meet not as we parted."]	388
THE ISLE	390

INTRODUCTION.

THE selection from Shelley's poems now offered to the public has not been framed upon the principle of an anthology. The criterion adopted has in most instances been simply the length of the pieces. It is thus practically a reissue of a precious little volume, long ago worn to pieces in the pocket of many an admirer of Shelley, Moxon's edition of Shelley's Minor Poems. The writer has to express his sincere approval of the general principle of procedure in regard to this treasury of "infinite riches in a little room," notwithstanding some reservation of opinion on points of detail. One powerful motive for applying it to Shelley is the circumstance that he is almost the only poet to whom it can be applied at all. Where else shall we find the poet whose minor poems can be

INTRODUCTION.

taken up in the mass and printed almost without retrenchment, in the perfect assurance that the result will be as truly a book of beauties as if the entire body of his writings had been sifted for this purpose? An indiscriminate collection of all the minor pieces of even such poets as Coleridge, Goethe, or Heine, would be a valuable book indeed, but by no means a book of beauties. One exception there is, and many will be surprised to learn that it is Wordsworth. This great poet has suffered almost as much from the common-place of criticism as Shelley: his prosiness is almost as much an article of faith as Shelley's obscurity and lack of human interest. Yet, as a matter of fact, when in 1857 Mr. William Johnston reprinted the minor poems produced by Wordsworth during a quarter of a century, he found it necessary to omit only three as deficient in the quality of poetry. It is interesting to trace this point of analogy between writers who have more affinity than is surmised by the exclusive worshippers of the elder of them.

INTRODUCTION.

Apart from this consideration, the publication of a particular class of Shelley's poems on the principle adopted here, may be justified by the great difficulty of forming a satisfactory selection on any other. Selection from the entire works of any great author, except when confined to aphoristic or sententious passages, is indeed at best an unsatisfactory business:

> "As if a child in glee,
> Catching the flakes of the salt froth,
> Cried, 'Look, my mother, here's the sea.'"

But in Shelley's case peculiar difficulties present themselves. What is to be rejected? For a writer of such intensity, he is singularly equable and sustained. The height to which he ascends is hardly more remarkable than the length of his sojourn at it. Except for the fourth act of "Prometheus Unbound," which was avowedly added as an after-thought, it is difficult to point out any section of his longer poems as distinctly inferior, or by consequence any as markedly superior, to the rest. This signal exception to the *aliquando bonus dormitat Homerus* axiom, is no doubt not to be

INTRODUCTION.

so much ascribed to an intrinsic superiority over other great writers less characterized by uniformity of elevation, as to the essentially lyrical character of his genius.

Continuity of inspiration, implying continuity of excellence, is an indispensable condition of success in lyrical poetry: the peculiarity with Shelley was that the impulse which others would have exhausted in a song carried him through an epic or a drama. In consequence, the passages most easily detached from the context are generally those least suggestive of the general spirit of the poem. An anthologist culling from the "Revolt of Islam," for example, would be likely to select the descriptions of Cythna (Canto II., stanzas 21-32); and of the child who ministers to the fallen tyrant (Canto V., stanzas 21-31). These two exquisite pictures of childish innocence, nevertheless, afford but an imperfect conception of that lurid and stormy sublimity—

"As when some great painter dips
His pencil in the hues of earthquake and eclipse;"

or of that impassioned love of liberty, which

constitute the distinctive notes of the "Revolt of Islam." If justice is to be done to these, and at the same time to those episodical beauties which no editor could pass without a pang, the poem will claim more than its share of space, and the same difficulty will recur with every composition of any considerable length. Hence, although the task of selection is most fascinating to every person endowed with a taste for poetry, and one which no such person can perform without accomplishing something excellent, it seems better on the whole to pursue the more modest course adopted here. Even this affords a field for the exercise of taste and skill, on which the editor might have adventured himself. It was not absolutely necessary to adhere to the strictly chronological order of the poems. They might have been grouped so as to lead imperceptibly from one phase of the poet's mind to another, and to form collectively but a single poem; or they might have been made to enhance each other's splendour by contrast, like jewels in a diadem, instead of being, like the flowers in "The Question," presented in the order in which they originally had birth. The present writer is free to confess that he could hardly have resisted such a temptation. Fortunately, perhaps, the decision has not rested with him, and the reader has, at all events, the advantage of perusing the pieces in the chronological sequence which most perfectly illustrates the development of the poet's art, in so far as development is predicable of a career of such brevity. These remarks may be fitly succeeded by some observations on this point—previously, however, it may be desirable to advert to the presence of some particular pieces in the text, and the general relation of the collection to its predecessor.

It will at once occur to the reader already versed in Shelley, that several of the poems comprehended in this selection are "minor" merely in respect of length. "Alastor," which is included, is in every respect a more important piece than "Rosalind and Helen," which is omitted. "Epipsychidion" and

INTRODUCTION.

"Adonais" claim fully as large a space in the field of English literature as "Lamia" and "The Eve of St. Agnes," which no one would think of classing among Keats's "minor poems." The definition must therefore be accepted with a certain latitude, but may be thought to be warranted by the precedent of the editor of Moxon's edition, by whom the nine longest pieces ("Alastor," "The Witch of Atlas," "Epipsychidion," "Julian and Maddalo," "Lines written among the Euganean Hills," "The Masque of Anarchy," "Adonais," "The Sensitive Plant," and "The Triumph of Life") are placed at the head of the volume, the remainder being arranged chronologically, under the heads "Early Poems" and "Miscellaneous Poems." The present arrangement is chronological throughout. To the writer the original order appears preferable, and he would have extended it so far as to embrace the "Letter to Maria Gisborne." The abrupt transition from long to shorter poems suggests an unevenness infinitesimal indeed, but still to be avoided when all else is so dainty and exquisite. The same consideration fully justifies the disappearance of "The Masque of Anarchy" and one or two slighter pieces inspired by political animosity. It is less easy to account for the omission of "The Triumph of Life," so much more legitimately ranked among "minor poems" than "Epipsychidion," or "The Witch of Atlas." Surely not merely because it is incomplete? Yet it would seem so, for no other motive can be surmised for the omission of "A Vision of the Sea," which the author nevertheless deemed sufficiently complete for publication in his lifetime. The procedure of the two editions is diametrically opposite as respects the lyrical passages of "Hellas." The former gives all except the first, the latter the first only. All should be given or none, and painful as it is to turn aside from such examples of the highest lyrical inspiration, it is difficult to find a reason for their insertion which would not equally justify that of the corresponding passages in "Prometheus." A more important divergence is that while Moxon's edition gives the first two cantos of "Queen Mab" according to the original text, under the fancy title of "Ianthe," this one presents Shelley's own revision of it—as for the first time fully and accurately printed by Mr. Buxton Forman—under his own title of "The Dæmon of the World." The reasons which dictate adherence to the text of the original "Queen Mab" in Shelley's collected works, are equally conclusive in favour of the abridged recension in an edition of his minor pieces. Its publication here, it may be anticipated, will be especially welcome to those readers of Shelley who do not happen to possess the editions containing "The Dæmon of the World." They will now have the opportunity for a most instructive comparison between Shelley's first and second thoughts. He evidently laboured to modify the originally didactic character of the poem, but οὐδέποτ' ἂν θείης λεῖον τὸν τραχὺν ἐχῖνον.

This tendency is indeed characteristic of Shelley's poetical development in general, which reverses that of most poets. It is usual to begin as a simple minstrel, and to end as the exponent of a system. Stuart Mill, and in this instance most wisely, advised Mr. Tennyson "to render his poetic endowment the means of giving impressiveness to important truths." Shelley had prematurely begun where Mr. Mill would have had him end. The most imaginative of writers, the man who within five years produced more pure, essential, sublimated poetry, more verse solely depending for its acceptance upon its mere poetic quality, than all his contemporaries put together—this man began his career as the apostle of a system of thought. "Queen Mab" is a didactic poem, and at a much later date we find the author professing that he "considers poetry very subordinate to moral science;" though, in his "Defence of Poetry," he ultimately recants this opinion. The history of his composition is thus that of the gradual retrogression of the didactic element, which "the years that bring the philosophic mind" would probably have reinstated, but which, as we actually have him, seems to wane away until it is almost in abeyance. The student of this little volume will remark the increasing preponderance of the lyrical element, and the constant tendency towards an absolute simplicity both of thought and execution. Previously to 1819, the strictly lyrical pieces are neither numerous nor, with one or two signal exceptions, important. The poet's energies are chiefly engrossed by his "Revolt of Islam" and "Prometheus Unbound," poems with a purpose, although the purpose is almost eclipsed by the poetry. Even in 1820 he produces his "Ode to Liberty" and "Ode to Naples," magnificent but elaborated compositions, related to his simpler strains as Turner's landscapes painted in emulation of Claude are to his water-colour drawings. In the last years of his life his lyrics become more and more utterances of personal emotion, and are more and more characterized by simplicity of thought and transparency of diction. The slightest circumstance, a country walk, a plant in a casement, the tinkle of a guitar, is sufficient foundation for a lyric not less impassioned, if more subdued in expression, than that erewhile consecrated to "the breath of Autumn's being." The modification may be illustrated by a comparison of two poems allied in sentiment, the "Stanzas written in Dejection" (1818); and "Rarely, rarely comest thou" (1821). In the first, style and melody divide attention with the feeling; sympathy is almost impaired by admiration. In the second, style and melody, though not really less exquisite, are hardly observed; and the felicity of the diction is almost concealed by its appropriateness. It is time to acknowledge that the poet who most absolutely wielded the verbal and metrical resources of his mother-tongue, was also the most perfect master of poetical simplicity it has possessed, and that the very end and aim of his training seems to have been to make him so.

The care bestowed upon this selection by its original framer needs no comment. Mr.

INTRODUCTION.

Forman's text has been followed throughout. Recently discovered poems, such as the exquisite "Lines in the Bay of Lerici," have been inserted, and the titles of others rendered agreeable to Shelley's intention. In some instances this is very important; thus the lines at p. 347, and at p. 30, gain greatly in beauty and effectiveness by being known to be respectively addressed to Edward Williams and to Coleridge. The latter address is a remarkable instance of Shelley's psychological insight. Coleridge would not have written otherwise about himself.

In conclusion, the hope may be expressed that a selection so well adapted for a wide circulation as the present may contribute to render Shelley a popular poet. The existing estrangement of the highest poetry from popular sympathy is equally to be regretted in the interest of the poet and his nation. The former cannot attain the full measure of his fame and influence until his words are household words: it is ill for the latter when its best minds are among it, but not of it.

INTRODUCTION.

Poets and readers have alike been in fault: some men of genius have wilfully chosen eccentric themes, or exhausted themselves in mere *tours de force;* while the deficient cultivation of the general public would restrict efforts made solely on its behalf to a very narrow area. But more in fault than either is the "false medium" of stereotyped criticism which interposes between the two. The great poets of the early part of this century—long after they have proved themselves, in Shelley's own fine phrase, "the unacknowledged legislators of the world"—are, from the force of tradition, treated as if they were still under the ferule of Gifford or Jeffrey. The reader who comes to them with a fresh mind will discover that this is cant in its primary sense, not of hypocrisy, but of unthinking repetition. Wordsworth is not, with occasional exceptions, prosaic, or Coleridge indistinct, or Keats merely sensuous, or Shelley deficient in human interest or feeling. The only possible foundation for such a charge is, that—except in the "Cenci"—he does not embody his conceptions in personages derived from history or his own observation of life. Neither does Spenser, and Shelley is Spenser and Sappho too. Most of the other standard objections to his poetry proceed from mere inability to keep pace with a nimble and subtle intelligence, even when no remarkable intellectual effort seems to be required. A recent censor of the "Ode to the West Wind," for example, reproves Shelley for comparing leaves to ghosts, though he would have suffered him to compare ghosts to leaves. The same instinctive aversion to anything original has unconsciously inspired many another criticism of similar calibre. The only other serious obstacles to the general comprehension of Shelley are his erudition and the Italian atmosphere which envelops much of his poetry. Even these are less formidable than that dependence on local associations which, beyond the precincts of these islands, will probably be found to overbalance all the weighty claims to an European reputation preferred on Wordsworth's behalf by his latest editor.

Shelley is at all events cosmopolitan: his fame may in the long run be rather promoted than impeded by its association with literatures and mythologies which have become imperishable constituents of human culture, and with regions of the earth so renowned as to be in a manner familiar to those who have never beheld them. This much may be affirmed, that Shelley's hopes of ultimate enrolment among the select band of the supreme poets of the world rest upon the same foundation as the hopes of the world itself. Enlightenment and the enthusiasm of humanity will always insure him readers: prevalent barbarism or materialism would extinguish him more speedily and effectually than any other writer.

R. GARNETT.

November 12, 1879.

ALASTOR;

OR,

THE SPIRIT OF SOLITUDE.

EARTH, ocean, air, belovèd brotherhood !
If our great Mother has imbued my soul
With aught of natural piety to feel
Your love, and recompense the boon with mine ;
If dewy morn, and odorous noon, and even,
With sunset and its gorgeous ministers,
And solemn midnight's tingling silentness ;
If autumn's hollow sighs in the sere wood,
And winter robing with pure snow and crowns
Of starry ice the gray grass and bare boughs ;
If spring's voluptuous pantings when she breathes
Her first sweet kisses, have been dear to me ;
If no bright bird, insect, or gentle beast
I consciously have injured, but still loved
And cherished these my kindred ; then forgive
This boast, belovèd brethren, and withdraw
No portion of your wonted favour now !

Mother of this unfathomable world !
Favour my solemn song, for I have loved
Thee ever, and thee only ; I have watched
Thy shadow, and the darkness of thy steps,
And my heart ever gazes on the depth
Of thy deep mysteries. I have made my bed
In charnels and on coffins, where black death
Keeps record of the trophies won from thee,
Hoping to still these obstinate questionings
Of thee and thine, by forcing some lone ghost
Thy messenger, to render up the tale
Of what we are. In lone and silent hours,
When night makes a weird sound of its own stillness,
Like an inspired and desperate alchymist
Staking his very life on some dark hope,
Have I mixed awful talk and asking looks
With my most innocent love, until strange tears
Uniting with those breathless kisses, made
Such magic as compels the charmèd night
To render up thy charge : . . . and, though ne'er yet
Thou hast unveiled thy inmost sanctuary,
Enough from incommunicable dream,
And twilight phantasms, and deep noonday thought,
Has shone within me, that serenely now
And moveless, as a long-forgotten lyre
Suspended in the solitary dome

THE SPIRIT OF SOLITUDE.

Of some mysterious and deserted fane,
I wait thy breath, Great Parent, that my strain
May modulate with murmurs of the air,
And motions of the forests and the sea,
And voice of living beings, and woven hymns
Of night and day, and the deep heart of man.

  There was a Poet whose untimely tomb
No human hands with pious reverence reared,
But the charmed eddies of autumnal winds
Built o'er his mouldering bones a pyramid
Of mouldering leaves in the waste wilderness : —
A lovely youth, — no mourning maiden decked
With weeping flowers, or votive cypress wreath,
The lone couch of his everlasting sleep : —
Gentle, and brave, and generous, — no lorn bard
Breathed o'er his dark fate one melodious sigh :
He lived, he died, he sung, in solitude.
Strangers have wept to hear his passionate notes,
And virgins, as unknown he past, have pined
And wasted for fond love of his wild eyes.
The fire of those soft orbs has ceased to burn,
And Silence, too enamoured of that voice,
Locks its mute music in her rugged cell.

By solemn vision, and bright silver dream,
His infancy was nurtured. Every sight
And sound from the vast earth and ambient air,
Sent to his heart its choicest impulses.
The fountains of divine philosophy
Fled not his thirsting lips, and all of great,
Or good, or lovely, which the sacred past
In truth or fable consecrates, he felt
And knew. When early youth had past, he left
His cold fireside and alienated home
To seek strange truths in undiscovered lands.
Many a wide waste and tangled wilderness
Has lured his fearless steps; and he has bought
With his sweet voice and eyes, from savage men,
His rest and food. Nature's most secret steps
He like her shadow has pursued, where'er
The red volcano overcanopies
Its fields of snow and pinnacles of ice
With burning smoke, or where bitumen lakes
On black bare pointed islets ever beat
With sluggish surge, or where the secret caves
Rugged and dark, winding among the springs
Of fire and poison, inaccessible
To avarice or pride, their starry domes
Of diamond and of gold expand above
Numberless and immeasurable halls,

Frequent with crystal column, and clear shrines
Of pearl, and thrones radiant with chrysolite.
Nor had that scene of ampler majesty
Than gems or gold, the varying roof of heaven
And the green earth lost in his heart its claims
To love and wonder; he would linger long
In lonesome vales, making the wild his home,
Until the doves and squirrels would partake
From his innocuous hand his bloodless food,
Lured by the gentle meaning of his looks,
And the wild antelope, that starts whene'er
The dry leaf rustles in the brake, suspend
Her timid steps to gaze upon a form
More graceful than her own.

                              His wandering step
Obedient to high thoughts, has visited
The awful ruins of the days of old:
Athens, and Tyre, and Balbec, and the waste
Where stood Jerusalem, the fallen towers
Of Babylon, the eternal pyramids,
Memphis and Thebes, and whatsoe'er of strange
Sculptured on alabaster obelisk,
Or jasper tomb, or mutilated sphynx,
Dark Æthiopia in her desert hills
Conceals. Among the ruined temples there,

Stupendous columns, and wild images
Of more than man, where marble dæmons watch
The Zodiac's brazen mystery, and dead men
Hang their mute thoughts on the mute walls around,
He lingered, poring on memorials
Of the world's youth, through the long burning day
Gazed on those speechless shapes, nor, when the moon
Filled the mysterious halls with floating shades
Suspended he that task, but ever gazed
And gazed, till meaning on his vacant mind
Flashed like strong inspiration, and he saw
The thrilling secrets of the birth of time.

    Meanwhile an Arab maiden brought his food,
Her daily portion, from her father's tent,
And spread her matting for his couch, and stole
From duties and repose to tend his steps : —
Enamoured, yet not daring for deep awe
To speak her love : — and watched his nightly sleep,
Sleepless herself, to gaze upon his lips
Parted in slumber, whence the regular breath
Of innocent dreams arose : then, when red morn
Made paler the pale moon, to her cold home
Wildered, and wan, and panting, she returned.

THE SPIRIT OF SOLITUDE.

The Poet wandering on, through Arabie
And Persia, and the wild Carmanian waste,
And o'er the aërial mountains which pour down
Indus and Oxus from their icy caves,
In joy and exultation held his way;
Till in the vale of Cashmire, far within
Its loneliest dell, where odorous plants entwine
Beneath the hollow rocks a natural bower,
Beside a sparkling rivulet he stretched
His languid limbs. A vision on his sleep
There came, a dream of hopes that never yet
Had flushed his cheek. He dreamed a veilèd maid
Sate near him, talking in low solemn tones.
Her voice was like the voice of his own soul
Heard in the calm of thought; its music long,
Like woven sounds of streams and breezes, held
His inmost sense suspended in its web
Of many-coloured woof and shifting hues.
Knowledge and truth and virtue were her theme,
And lofty hopes of divine liberty,
Thoughts the most dear to him, and poesy,
Herself a poet. Soon the solemn mood
Of her pure mind kindled through all her frame
A permeating fire: wild numbers then
She raised, with voice stifled in tremulous sobs
Subdued by its own pathos: her fair hands

Were bare alone, sweeping from some strange harp
Strange symphony, and in their branching veins
The eloquent blood told an ineffable tale.
The beating of her heart was heard to fill
The pauses of her music, and her breath
Tumultuously accorded with those fits
Of intermitted song. Sudden she rose,
As if her heart impatiently endured
Its bursting burthen : at the sound he turned,
And saw by the warm light of their own life
Her glowing limbs beneath the sinuous veil
Of woven wind, her outspread arms now bare,
Her dark locks floating in the breath of night,
Her beamy bending eyes, her parted lips
Outstretched, and pale, and quivering eagerly.
His strong heart sunk and sickened with excess
Of love. He reared his shuddering limbs and quelled
His gasping breath, and spread his arms to meet
Her panting bosom : . . . she drew back a while,
Then, yielding to the irresistible joy,
With frantic gesture and short breathless cry
Folded his frame in her dissolving arms.
Now blackness veiled his dizzy eyes, and night
Involved and swallowed up the vision ; sleep,
Like a dark flood suspended in its course,
Rolled back its impulse on his vacant brain.

Roused by the shock he started from his trance —
The cold white light of morning, the blue moon
Low in the west, the clear and garish hills,
The distinct valley and the vacant woods,
Spread round him where he stood. Whither have fled
The hues of heaven that canopied his bower
Of yesternight? The sounds that soothed his sleep,
The mystery and the majesty of Earth,
The joy, the exultation? His wan eyes
Gaze on the empty scene as vacantly
As ocean's moon looks on the moon in heaven.
The spirit of sweet human love has sent
A vision to the sleep of him who spurned
Her choicest gifts. He eagerly pursues
Beyond the realms of dream that fleeting shade;
He overleaps the bounds. Alas! alas!
Were limbs, and breath, and being intertwined
Thus treacherously? Lost, lost, for ever lost,
In the wide pathless desert of dim sleep,
That beautiful shape! Does the dark gate of death
Conduct to thy mysterious paradise,
O Sleep? Does the bright arch of rainbow clouds,
And pendent mountains seen in the calm lake,
Lead only to a black and watery depth,
While death's blue vault, with loathliest vapours hung,
Where every shade which the foul grave exhales

Hides its dead eye from the detested day,
Conduct, O Sleep, to thy delightful realms?
This doubt with sudden tide flowed on his heart,
The insatiate hope which it awakened, stung
His brain even like despair.

                        While day-light held
The sky, the Poet kept mute conference
With his still soul. At night the passion came,
Like the fierce fiend of a distempered dream,
And shook him from his rest, and led him forth
Into the darkness.—As an eagle grasped
In folds of the green serpent, feels her breast
Burn with the poison, and precipitates
Through night and day, tempest, and calm, and cloud,
Frantic with dizzying anguish, her blind flight
O'er the wide aëry wilderness: thus driven
By the bright shadow of that lovely dream,
Beneath the cold glare of the desolate night,
Through tangled swamps and deep precipitous dells,
Startling with careless step the moon-light snake,
He fled. Red morning dawned upon his flight,
Shedding the mockery of its vital hues
Upon his cheek of death. He wandered on
Till vast Aornos seen from Petra's steep
Hung o'er the low horizon like a cloud;

Through Balk, and where the desolated tombs
Of Parthian kings scatter to every wind
Their wasting dust, wildly he wandered on,
Day after day, a weary waste of hours,
Bearing within his life the brooding care
That ever fed on its decaying flame.
And now his limbs were lean; his scattered hair
Sered by the autumn of strange suffering
Sung dirges in the wind; his listless hand
Hung like dead bone within its withered skin;
Life, and the lustre that consumed it, shone
As in a furnace burning secretly
From his dark eyes alone. The cottagers,
Who ministered with human charity
His human wants, beheld with wondering awe
Their fleeting visitant. The mountaineer,
Encountering on some dizzy precipice
That spectral form, deemed that the Spirit of wind
With lightning eyes, and eager breath, and feet
Disturbing not the drifted snow, had paused
In its career: the infant would conceal
His troubled visage in his mother's robe
In terror at the glare of those wild eyes,
To remember their strange light in many a dream
Of after-times; but youthful maidens, taught
By nature, would interpret half the woe

That wasted him, would call him with false names
Brother, and friend, would press his pallid hand
At parting, and watch, dim through tears, the path
Of his departure from their father's door.

   At length upon the lone Chorasmian shore
He paused, a wide and melancholy waste
Of putrid marshes. A strong impulse urged
His steps to the sea-shore. A swan was there,
Beside a sluggish stream among the reeds.
It rose as he approached, and with strong wings
Scaling the upward sky, bent its bright course
High over the immeasurable main.
His eyes pursued its flight.—"Thou hast a home,
Beautiful bird; thou voyagest to thine home,
Where thy sweet mate will twine her downy neck
With thine, and welcome thy return with eyes
Bright in the lustre of their own fond joy.
And what am I that I should linger here,
With voice far sweeter than thy dying notes,
Spirit more vast than thine, frame more attuned
To beauty, wasting these surpassing powers
In the deaf air, to the blind earth, and heaven
That echoes not my thoughts?" A gloomy smile
Of desperate hope wrinkled his quivering lips.
For sleep, he knew, kept most relentlessly

THE SPIRIT OF SOLITUDE.

Its precious charge, and silent death exposed,
Faithless perhaps as sleep, a shadowy lure,
With doubtful smile mocking its own strange charms.

   Startled by his own thoughts he looked around.
There was no fair fiend near him, not a sight
Or sound of awe but in his own deep mind.
A little shallop floating near the shore
Caught the impatient wandering of his gaze.
It had been long abandoned, for its sides
Gaped wide with many a rift, and its frail joints
Swayed with the undulations of the tide.
A restless impulse urged him to embark
And meet lone Death on the drear ocean's waste;
For well he knew that mighty Shadow loves
The slimy caverns of the populous deep.

   The day was fair and sunny, sea and sky
Drank its inspiring radiance, and the wind
Swept strongly from the shore, blackening the waves.
Following his eager soul, the wanderer
Leaped in the boat, he spread his cloak aloft
On the bare mast, and took his lonely seat,
And felt the boat speed o'er the tranquil sea
Like a torn cloud before the hurricane.

As one that in a silver vision floats
Obedient to the sweep of odorous winds
Upon resplendent clouds, so rapidly
Along the dark and ruffled waters fled
The straining boat.—A whirlwind swept it on,
With fierce gusts and precipitating force,
Through the white ridges of the chafèd sea.
The waves arose. Higher and higher still
Their fierce necks writhed beneath the tempest's sco
Like serpents struggling in a vulture's grasp.
Calm and rejoicing in the fearful war
Of wave ruining on wave, and blast on blast
Descending, and black flood on whirlpool driven
With dark obliterating course, he sate :
As if their genii were the ministers
Appointed to conduct him to the light
Of those belovèd eyes, the Poet sate
Holding the steady helm. Evening came on,
The beams of sunset hung their rainbow hues
High 'mid the shifting domes of sheeted spray
That canopied his path o'er the waste deep ;
Twilight, ascending slowly from the east,
Entwined in duskier wreaths her braided locks
O'er the fair front and radiant eyes of day ;
Night followed, clad with stars. On every side
More horribly the multitudinous streams

Of ocean's mountainous waste to mutual war
Rushed in dark tumult thundering, as to mock
The calm and spangled sky. The little boat
Still fled before the storm; still fled, like foam
Down the steep cataract of a wintry river;
Now pausing on the edge of the riven wave;
Now leaving far behind the bursting mass
That fell, convulsing ocean. Safely fled—
As if that frail and wasted human form,
Had been an elemental god.

                              At midnight
The moon arose: and lo! the etherial cliffs
Of Caucasus, whose icy summits shone
Among the stars like sunlight, and around
Whose caverned base the whirlpools and the waves
Bursting and eddying irresistibly
Rage and resound for ever.—Who shall save?—
The boat fled on,—the boiling torrent drove,—
The crags closed round with black and jaggèd arms,
The shattered mountain overhung the sea,
And faster still, beyond all human speed,
Suspended on the sweep of the smooth wave,
The little boat was driven. A cavern there
Yawned, and amid its slant and winding depths
Ingulphed the rushing sea. The boat fled on

With unrelaxing speed.—'Vision and Love!'
The Poet cried aloud, 'I have beheld
The path of thy departure. Sleep and death
Shall not divide us long!'

       The boat pursued
The windings of the cavern. Day-light shone
At length upon that gloomy river's flow;
Now, where the fiercest war among the waves
Is calm, on the unfathomable stream
The boat moves slowly. Where the mountain, riven,
Exposed those black depths to the azure sky,
Ere yet the flood's enormous volume fell
Even to the base of Caucasus, with sound
That shook the everlasting rocks, the mass
Filled with one whirlpool all that ample chasm;
Stair above stair the eddying waters rose,
Circling immeasurably fast, and laved
With alternating dash the knarlèd roots
Of mighty trees, that stretched their giant arms
In darkness over it. I' the midst was left,
Reflecting, yet distorting every cloud,
A pool of treacherous and tremendous calm.
Seized by the sway of the ascending stream,
With dizzy swiftness, round, and round, and round,
Ridge after ridge the straining boat arose,

Till on the verge of the extremest curve,
Where, through an opening of the rocky bank,
The waters overflow, and a smooth spot
Of glassy quiet mid those battling tides
Is left, the boat paused shuddering.—Shall it sink
Down the abyss? Shall the reverting stress
Of that resistless gulph embosom it?
Now shall it fall?—A wandering stream of wind,
Breathed from the west, has caught the expanded sail,
And, lo! with gentle motion, between banks
Of mossy slope, and on a placid stream,
Beneath a woven grove it sails, and, hark!
The ghastly torrent mingles its far roar,
With the breeze murmuring in the musical woods.
Where the embowering trees recede, and leave
A little space of green expanse, the cove
Is closed by meeting banks, whose yellow flowers
For ever gaze on their own drooping eyes,
Reflected in the crystal calm. The wave
Of the boat's motion marred their pensive task,
Which nought but vagrant bird, or wanton wind,
Or falling spear-grass, or their own decay
Had e'er disturbed before. The Poet longed
To deck with their bright hues his withered hair,
But on his heart its solitude returned,
And he forbore. Not the strong impulse hid

In those flushed cheeks, bent eyes, and shadowy frame
Had yet performed its ministry: it hung
Upon his life, as lightning in a cloud
Gleams, hovering ere it vanish, ere the floods
Of night close over it.

      The noonday sun
Now shone upon the forest, one vast mass
Of mingling shade, whose brown magnificence
A narrow vale embosoms. There, huge caves,
Scooped in the dark base of their aëry rocks
Mocking its moans, respond and roar for ever.
The meeting boughs and implicated leaves
Wove twilight o'er the Poet's path, as led
By love, or dream, or god, or mightier Death,
He sought in Nature's dearest haunt, some bank,
Her cradle, and his sepulchre. More dark
And dark the shades accumulate. The oak,
Expanding its immense and knotty arms,
Embraces the light beech. The pyramids
Of the tall cedar overarching, frame
Most solemn domes within, and far below,
Like clouds suspended in an emerald sky,
The ash and the acacia floating hang
Tremulous and pale. Like restless serpents, clothed
In rainbow and in fire, the parasites,

Starred with ten thousand blossoms, flow around
The gray trunks, and, as gamesome infants' eyes,
With gentle meanings, and most innocent wiles,
Fold their beams round the hearts of those that love,
These twine their tendrils with the wedded boughs
Uniting their close union ; the woven leaves
Make net-work of the dark blue light of day,
And the night's noontide clearness, mutable
As shapes in the weird clouds. Soft mossy lawns
Beneath these canopies extend their swells,
Fragrant with perfumed herbs, and eyed with blooms
Minute yet beautiful. One darkest glen
Sends from its woods of musk-rose, twined with jasmine,
A soul-dissolving odour, to invite
To some more lovely mystery. Through the dell,
Silence and Twilight here, twin-sisters, keep
Their noonday watch, and sail among the shades,
Like vaporous shapes half seen ; beyond, a well,
Dark, gleaming, and of most translucent wave,
Images all the woven boughs above,
And each depending leaf, and every speck
Of azure sky, darting between their chasms ;
Nor aught else in the liquid mirror laves
Its portraiture, but some inconstant star
Between one foliaged lattice twinkling fair,
Or, painted bird, sleeping beneath the moon,

Or gorgeous insect floating motionless,
Unconscious of the day, ere yet his wings
Have spread their glories to the gaze of noon.

    Hither the Poet came. His eyes beheld
Their own wan light through the reflected lines
Of his thin hair, distinct in the dark depth
Of that still fountain ; as the human heart,
Gazing in dreams over the gloomy grave,
Sees its own treacherous likeness there. He heard
The motion of the leaves, the grass that sprung
Startled and glanced and trembled even to feel
An unaccustomed presence, and the sound
Of the sweet brook that from the secret springs
Of that dark fountain rose. A Spirit seemed
To stand beside him — clothed in no bright robes
Of shadowy silver or enshrining light,
Borrowed from aught the visible world affords
Of grace, or majesty, or mystery ; —
But, undulating woods, and silent well,
And leaping rivulet, and evening gloom
Now deepening the dark shades, for speech assuming,
Held commune with him, as if he and it
Were all that was, — only . . . when his regard
Was raised by intense pensiveness, . . . two eyes,
Two starry eyes, hung in the gloom of thought,

And seemed with their serene and azure smiles
To beckon him.

                Obedient to the light
That shone within his soul, he went, pursuing
The windings of the dell.—The rivulet
Wanton and wild, through many a green ravine
Beneath the forest flowed. Sometimes it fell
Among the moss with hollow harmony
Dark and profound. Now on the polished stones
It danced; like childhood laughing as it went:
Then, through the plain in tranquil wanderings crept,
Reflecting every herb and drooping bud
That overhung its quietness.—'O stream!
Whose source is inaccessibly profound,
Whither do thy mysterious waters tend?
Thou imagest my life. Thy darksome stillness,
Thy dazzling waves, thy loud and hollow gulphs,
Thy searchless fountain, and invisible course
Have each their type in me: and the wide sky,
And measureless ocean may declare as soon
What oozy cavern or what wandering cloud
Contains thy waters, as the universe
Tell where these living thoughts reside, when stretched
Upon thy flowers my bloodless limbs shall waste
I' the passing wind!'

                            Beside the grassy shore
Of the small stream he went; he did impress
On the green moss his tremulous step, that caught
Strong shuddering from his burning limbs. As one
Roused by some joyous madness from the couch
Of fever, he did move; yet, not like him,
Forgetful of the grave, where, when the flame
Of his frail exultation shall be spent,
He must descend. With rapid steps he went
Beneath the shade of trees, beside the flow
Of the wild babbling rivulet; and now
The forest's solemn canopies were changed
For the uniform and lightsome evening sky.
Gray rocks did peep from the spare moss, and stemmed
The struggling brook: tall spires of windlestrae
Threw their thin shadows down the rugged slope,
And nought but knarlèd roots of ancient pines
Branchless and blasted, clenched with grasping roots
The unwilling soil. A gradual change was here,
Yet ghastly. For, as fast years flow away,
The smooth brow gathers, and the hair grows thin
And white, and where irradiate dewy eyes
Had shone, gleam stony orbs:—so from his steps
Bright flowers departed, and the beautiful shade
Of the green groves, with all their odorous winds
And musical motions. Calm, he still pursued

The stream, that with a larger volume now
Rolled through the labyrinthine dell; and there
Fretted a path through its descending curves
With its wintry speed. On every side now rose
Rocks, which, in unimaginable forms,
Lifted their black and barren pinnacles
In the light of evening, and its precipice
Obscuring the ravine, disclosed above,
Mid toppling stones, black gulphs and yawning caves,
Whose windings gave ten thousand various tongues
To the loud stream. Lo! where the pass expands
Its stony jaws, the abrupt mountain breaks,
And seems, with its accumulated crags,
To overhang the world: for wide expand
Beneath the wan stars and descending moon
Islanded seas, blue mountains, mighty streams,
Dim tracts and vast, robed in the lustrous gloom
Of leaden-coloured even, and fiery hills
Mingling their flames with twilight, on the verge
Of the remote horizon. The near scene,
In naked and severe simplicity,
Made contrast with the universe. A pine,
Rock-rooted, stretched athwart the vacancy
Its swinging boughs, to each inconstant blast
Yielding one only response, at each pause
In most familiar cadence, with the howl

The thunder and the hiss of homeless streams
Mingling its solemn song, whilst the broad river,
Foaming and hurrying o'er its rugged path,
Fell into that immeasurable void
Scattering its waters to the passing winds.

Yet the gray precipice and solemn pine
And torrent, were not all;—one silent nook
Was there. Even on the edge of that vast mountain,
Upheld by knotty roots and fallen rocks,
It overlooked in its serenity
The dark earth, and the bending vault of stars.
It was a tranquil spot, that seemed to smile
Even in the lap of horror. Ivy clasped
The fissured stones with its entwining arms,
And did embower with leaves for ever green,
And berries dark, the smooth and even space
Of its inviolated floor, and here
The children of the autumnal whirlwind bore,
In wanton sport, those bright leaves, whose decay,
Red, yellow, or etherially pale,
Rivals the pride of summer. 'Tis the haunt
Of every gentle wind, whose breath can teach
The wilds to love tranquillity. One step,
One human step alone, has ever broken
The stillness of its solitude:—one voice

Alone inspired its echoes;—even that voice
Which hither came, floating among the winds,
And led the loveliest among human forms
To make their wild haunts the depository
Of all the grace and beauty that endued
Its motions, render up its majesty,
Scatter its music on the unfeeling storm,
And to the damp leaves and blue cavern mould,
Nurses of rainbow flowers and branching moss,
Commit the colours of that varying cheek,
That snowy breast, those dark and drooping eyes.

   The dim and hornèd moon hung low, and poured
A sea of lustre on the horizon's verge
That overflowed its mountains. Yellow mist
Filled the unbounded atmosphere, and drank
Wan moonlight even to fulness: not a star
Shone, not a sound was heard; the very winds,
Danger's grim playmates, on that precipice
Slept, clasped in his embrace.—O, storm of death!
Whose sightless speed divides this sullen night:
And thou, colossal Skeleton, that, still
Guiding its irresistible career
In thy devastating omnipotence,
Art king of this frail world, from the red field
Of slaughter, from the reeking hospital,

The patriot's sacred couch, the snowy bed
Of innocence, the scaffold and the throne,
A mighty voice invokes thee. Ruin calls
His brother Death. A rare and regal prey
He hath prepared, prowling around the world;
Glutted with which thou mayst repose, and men
Go to their graves like flowers or creeping worms,
Nor ever more offer at thy dark shrine
The unheeded tribute of a broken heart.

   When on the threshold of the green recess
The wanderer's footsteps fell, he knew that death
Was on him. Yet a little, ere it fled,
Did he resign his high and holy soul
To images of the majestic past,
That paused within his passive being now,
Like winds that bear sweet music, when they breathe
Through some dim latticed chamber. He did place
His pale lean hand upon the rugged trunk
Of the old pine. Upon an ivied stone
Reclined his languid head, his limbs did rest,
Diffused and motionless, on the smooth brink
Of that obscurest chasm;—and thus he lay,
Surrendering to their final impulses
The hovering powers of life. Hope and despair,
The torturers, slept; no mortal pain or fear

Marred his repose, the influxes of sense,
And his own being unalloyed by pain,
Yet feebler and more feeble, calmly fed
The stream of thought, till he lay breathing there
At peace, and faintly smiling:—his last sight
Was the great moon, which o'er the western line
Of the wide world her mighty horn suspended,
With whose dun beams inwoven darkness seemed
To mingle. Now upon the jaggèd hills
It rests, and still as the divided frame
Of the vast meteor sunk, the Poet's blood,
That ever beat in mystic sympathy
With nature's ebb and flow, grew feebler still:
And when two lessening points of light alone
Gleamed through the darkness, the alternate gasp
Of his faint respiration scarce did stir
The stagnate night:—till the minutest ray
Was quenched, the pulse yet lingered in his heart.
It paused—it fluttered. But when heaven remained
Utterly black, the murky shades involved
An image, silent, cold, and motionless,
As their own voiceless earth and vacant air.
Even as a vapour fed with golden beams
That ministered on sunlight, ere the west
Eclipses it, was now that wondrous frame—
No sense, no motion, no divinity—

A fragile lute, on whose harmonious strings
The breath of heaven did wander — a bright stream
Once fed with many-voicèd waves — a dream
Of youth, which night and time have quenched for ever,
Still, dark, and dry, and unremembered now.

   O, for Medea's wondrous alchemy,
Which wheresoe'er it fell made the earth gleam
With bright flowers, and the wintry boughs exhale
From vernal blooms fresh fragrance ! O, that God,
Profuse of poisons, would concede the chalice
Which but one living man has drained, who now,
Vessel of deathless wrath, a slave that feels
No proud exemption in the blighting curse
He bears, over the world wanders for ever,
Lone as incarnate death ! O, that the dream
Of dark magician in his visioned cave,
Raking the cinders of a crucible
For life and power, even when his feeble hand
Shakes in its last decay, were the true law
Of this so lovely world ! But thou art fled
Like some frail exhalation ; which the dawn
Robes in its golden beams, — ah ! thou hast fled !
The brave, the gentle, and the beautiful,
The child of grace and genius. Heartless things
Are done and said i' the world, and many worms

And beasts and men live on, and mighty Earth
From sea and mountain, city and wilderness,
In vesper low or joyous orison,
Lifts still its solemn voice :— but thou art fled—
Thou canst no longer know or love the shapes
Of this phantasmal scene, who have to thee
Been purest ministers, who are, alas !
Now thou art not. Upon those pallid lips
So sweet even in their silence, on those eyes
That image sleep in death, upon that form
Yet safe from the worm's outrage, let no tear
Be shed — not even in thought. Nor, when those hues
Are gone, and those divinest lineaments,
Worn by the senseless wind, shall live alone
In the frail pauses of this simple strain,
Let not high verse, mourning the memory
Of that which is no more, or painting's woe
Or sculpture, speak in feeble imagery
Their own cold powers. Art and eloquence,
And all the shews o' the world are frail and vain
To weep a loss that turns their lights to shade.
It is a woe too 'deep for tears,' when all
Is reft at once, when some surpassing Spirit,
Whose light adorned the world around it, leaves
Those who remain behind, not sobs or groans,
The passionate tumult of a clinging hope ;

But pale despair and cold tranquillity,
Nature's vast frame, the web of human things,
Birth and the grave, that are not as they were.

[To Coleridge.]

ΔΑΚΡΥΕΙ ΔΙΟΙΣΩ ΠΟΤΜΟΝ ΑΠΟΤΜΟΝ.

O! there are spirits of the air,
    And genii of the evening breeze,
And gentle ghosts, with eyes as fair
    As star-beams among twilight trees:—
Such lovely ministers to meet
Oft hast thou turned from men thy lonely feet.

With mountain winds, and babbling springs,
    And moonlight seas, that are the voice
Of these inexplicable things
    Thou didst hold commune, and rejoice
When they did answer thee; but they
Cast, like a worthless boon, thy love away.

And thou hast sought in starry eyes
    Beams that were never meant for thine,

TO COLERIDGE.

Another's wealth : — tame sacrifice
   To a fond faith ! still dost thou pine?
Still dost thou hope that greeting hands,
   Voice, looks, or lips, may answer thy demands?

Ah ! wherefore didst thou build thine hope
   On the false earth's inconstancy?
Did thine own mind afford no scope
   Of love, or moving thoughts to thee?
That natural scenes or human smiles
Could steal the power to wind thee in their wiles.

Yes, all the faithless smiles are fled
   Whose falsehood left thee broken-hearted ;
The glory of the moon is dead ;
   Night's ghosts and dreams have now departed ;
Thine own soul still is true to thee,
But changed to a foul fiend through misery.

This fiend, whose ghastly presence ever
   Beside thee like thy shadow hangs,
Dream not to chase ; — the mad endeavor
   Would scourge thee to severer pangs.
Be as thou art. Thy settled fate,
Dark as it is, all change would aggravate.

STANZAS. — APRIL, 1814.

Away! the moor is dark beneath the moon,
  Rapid clouds have drank the last pale beam of even:
Away! the gathering winds will call the darkness soon,
  And profoundest midnight shroud the serene lights of heaven.

Pause not! The time is past! Every voice cries, Away!
  Tempt not with one last tear thy friend's ungentle mood:
Thy lover's eye, so glazed and cold, dares not entreat thy stay:
  Duty and dereliction guide thee back to solitude.

Away, away! to thy sad and silent home;
  Pour bitter tears on its desolated hearth;
Watch the dim shades as like ghosts they go and come,
  And complicate strange webs of melancholy mirth.

The leaves of wasted autumn woods shall float around thine head:
  The blooms of dewy spring shall gleam beneath thy feet:

STANZAS.—APRIL, 1814.

But thy soul or this world must fade in the frost that
  binds the dead,
 Ere midnight's frown and morning's smile, ere thou
  and peace may meet.

The cloud shadows of midnight possess their own repose,
 For the weary winds are silent, or the moon is in the
  deep:
Some respite to its turbulence unresting ocean knows;
 Whatever moves, or toils, or grieves, hath its appointed
  sleep.

Thou in the grave shalt rest — yet till the phantoms flee
 Which that house and heath and garden made dear
  to thee erewhile,
Thy remembrance, and repentance, and deep musings
  are not free
 From the music of two voices and the light of one
  sweet smile.

MUTABILITY.

We are as clouds that veil the midnight moon;
   How restlessly they speed, and gleam, and quiver,
Streaking the darkness radiantly!—yet soon
   Night closes round, and they are lost for ever:

Or like forgotten lyres, whose dissonant strings
   Give various response to each varying blast,
To whose frail frame no second motion brings
   One mood or modulation like the last.

We rest.—A dream has power to poison sleep;
   We rise.—One wandering thought pollutes the day;
We feel, conceive or reason, laugh or weep;
   Embrace fond woe, or cast our cares away:

It is the same!—For, be it joy or sorrow,
   The path of its departure still is free:
Man's yesterday may ne'er be like his morrow;
   Nought may endure but Mutability.

THERE IS NO WORK, NOR DEVICE, NOR KNOWL-
EDGE, NOR WISDOM, IN THE GRAVE, WHITHER
THOU GOEST.
Ecclesiastes.

THE pale, the cold, and the moony smile
   Which the meteor beam of a starless night
Sheds on a lonely and sea-girt isle,
   Ere the dawning of morn's undoubted light,
Is the flame of life so fickle and wan
That flits round our steps till their strength is gone.

O man ! hold thee on in courage of soul
   Through the stormy shades of thy worldly way,
And the billows of cloud that around thee roll
   Shall sleep in the light of a wondrous day,
Where hell and heaven shall leave thee free
To the universe of destiny.

This world is the nurse of all we know,
   This world is the mother of all we feel,
And the coming of death is a fearful blow
   To a brain unencompassed with nerves of steel;
When all that we know, or feel, or see,
Shall pass like an unreal mystery.

The secret things of the grave are there,
　　Where all but this frame must surely be,
Though the fine-wrought eye and the wondrous ear
　　No longer will live to hear or to see
All that is great and all that is strange
In the boundless realm of unending change.

Who telleth a tale of unspeaking death?
　　Who lifteth the veil of what is to come?
Who painteth the shadows that are beneath
　　The wide-winding caves of the peopled tomb?
Or uniteth the hopes of what shall be
With the fears and the love for that which we see?

A SUMMER-EVENING CHURCH-YARD.

Lechlade, Gloucestershire.

The wind has swept from the wide atmosphere
Each vapour that obscured the sunset's ray;
And pallid evening twines its beaming hair
In duskier braids around the languid eyes of day:
Silence and twilight, unbeloved of men,
Creep hand in hand from yon obscurest glen.

A SUMMER-EVENING CHURCH-YARD.

They breathe their spells towards the departing day,
Encompassing the earth, air, stars, and sea;
Light, sound, and motion own the potent sway,
Responding to the charm with its own mystery.
The winds are still, or the dry church-tower grass
Knows not their gentle motions as they pass.

Thou too, aerial Pile! whose pinnacles
Point from one shrine like pyramids of fire,
Obeyest in silence their sweet solemn spells,
Clothing in hues of heaven thy dim and distant spire,
Around whose lessening and invisible height
Gather among the stars the clouds of night.

The dead are sleeping in their sepulchres:
And, mouldering as they sleep, a thrilling sound
Half sense, half thought, among the darkness stirs,
Breathed from their wormy beds all living things around,
And mingling with the still night and mute sky
Its awful hush is felt inaudibly.

Thus solemnized and softened, death is mild
And terrorless as this serenest night:
Here could I hope, like some enquiring child
Sporting on graves, that death did hide from human sight
Sweet secrets, or beside its breathless sleep
That loveliest dreams perpetual watch did keep.

TO WORDSWORTH.

Poet of Nature, thou hast wept to know
That things depart which never may return:
Childhood and youth, friendship and love's first glow,
Have fled like sweet dreams, leaving thee to mourn.
These common woes I feel. One loss is mine
Which thou too feel'st, yet I alone deplore.
Thou wert as a lone star, whose light did shine
On some frail bark in winter's midnight roar:
Thou hast like to a rock-built refuge stood
Above the blind and battling multitude:
In honored poverty thy voice did weave
Songs consecrate to truth and liberty,—
Deserting these, thou leavest me to grieve,
Thus having been, that thou shouldst cease to be.

THE DÆMON OF THE WORLD.

    How wonderful is Death,
    Death and his brother Sleep!
One pale as yonder wan and hornèd moon,
    With lips of lurid blue,
The other glowing like the vital morn,
    When throned on ocean's wave
    It breathes over the world:
Yet both so passing strange and wonderful!

Hath then the iron-sceptred Skeleton,
Whose reign is in the tainted sepulchres,
To the hell dogs that couch beneath his throne
Cast that fair prey? Must that divinest form,
Which love and admiration cannot view
Without a beating heart, whose azure veins
Steal like dark streams along a field of snow,
Whose outline is as fair as marble clothed
In light of some sublimest mind, decay?

Nor putrefaction's breath
Leave aught of this pure spectacle
    But loathsomeness and ruin?—
    Spare aught but a dark theme,
On which the lightest heart might moralize?
Or is it but that downy-wingèd slumbers
Have charmed their nurse coy Silence near her lids
    To watch their own repose?
    Will they, when morning's beam
    Flows through those wells of light,
Seek far from noise and day some western cave,
Where woods and streams with soft and pausing winds
    A lulling murmur weave?—

    Ianthe doth not sleep
    The dreamless sleep of death:
Nor in her moonlight chamber silently
Doth Henry hear her regular pulses throb,
    Or mark her delicate cheek
With interchange of hues mock the broad moon,
    Outwatching weary night,
    Without assured reward.
    Her dewy eyes are closed;
On their translucent lids, whose texture fine
Scarce hides the dark blue orbs that burn below
    With unapparent fire,

THE DÆMON OF THE WORLD.

The baby Sleep is pillowed:
Her golden tresses shade
The bosom's stainless pride,
Twining like tendrils of the parasite
　　Around a marble column.

Hark! whence that rushing sound?
'Tis like a wondrous strain that sweeps
　　Around a lonely ruin
When west winds sigh and evening waves respond
　　In whispers from the shore:
'Tis wilder than the unmeasured notes
Which from the unseen lyres of dells and groves
　　The genii of the breezes sweep.
Floating on waves of music and of light
The chariot of the Dæmon of the World
　　Descends in silent power:
Its shape reposed within: slight as some cloud
That catches but the palest tinge of day
　　When evening yields to night,
Bright as that fibrous woof when stars indue
　　Its transitory robe.
Four shapeless shadows bright and beautiful
Draw that strange car of glory, reins of light
Check their unearthly speed; they stop and fold
　　Their wings of braided air:

The Dæmon leaning from the etherial car
    Gazed on the slumbering maid.
Human eye hath ne'er beheld
A shape so wild, so bright, so beautiful,
As that which o'er the maiden's charmèd sleep
    Waving a starry wand,
    Hung like a mist of light.
Such sounds as breathed around like odorous winds
    Of wakening spring arose,
Filling the chamber and the moonlight sky.

Maiden, the world's supremest spirit
    Beneath the shadow of her wings
Folds all thy memory doth inherit
    From ruin of divinest things,
        Feelings that lure thee to betray,
        And light of thoughts that pass away.

For thou hast earned a mighty boon,
    The truths which wisest poets see
Dimly, thy mind may make its own,
    Rewarding its own majesty,
        Entranced in some diviner mood
        Of self-oblivious solitude.

Custom, and Faith, and Power thou spurnest;
    From hate and awe thy heart is free;
Ardent and pure as day thou burnest,
    For dark and cold mortality
        A living light, to cheer it long,
        The watch-fires of the world among.

Therefore from nature's inner shrine,
    Where gods and fiends in worship bend,
Majestic spirit, be it thine
    The flame to seize, the veil to rend,
        Where the vast snake Eternity
        In charmèd sleep doth ever lie.

All that inspires thy voice of love,
    Or speaks in thy unclosing eyes,
Or through thy frame doth burn or move,
    Or think or feel, awake, arise !
        Spirit, leave for mine and me
        Earth's unsubstantial mimicry !

It ceased, and from the mute and moveless frame
    A radiant spirit arose,
All beautiful in naked purity.
Robed in its human hues it did ascend,

Disparting as it went the silver clouds
It moved towards the car, and took its seat
    Beside the Dæmon shape.

Obedient to the sweep of aery song,
    The mighty ministers
Unfurled their prismy wings.
    The magic car moved on;
The night was fair, innumerable stars
    Studded heaven's dark blue vault;
    The eastern wave grew pale
    With the first smile of morn.

    The magic car moved on.
    From the swift sweep of wings
The atmosphere in flaming sparkles flew;
    And where the burning wheels
Eddied above the mountain's loftiest peak
    Was traced a line of lightning.
Now far above a rock the utmost verge
    Of the wide earth it flew,
The rival of the Andes, whose dark brow
    Frowned o'er the silver sea.

Far, far below the chariot's stormy path,
    Calm as a slumbering babe,

Tremendous ocean lay.
Its broad and silent mirror gave to view
    The pale and waning stars,
    The chariot's fiery track,
    And the grey light of morn
    Tinging those fleecy clouds
That cradled in their folds the infant dawn.
    The chariot seemed to fly
Through the abyss of an immense concave,
Radiant with million constellations, tinged
    With shades of infinite color,
    And semicircled with a belt
    Flashing incessant meteors.

    As they approached their goal,
The wingèd shadows seemed to gather speed.
The sea no longer was distinguished; earth
Appeared a vast and shadowy sphere, suspended
    In the black concave of heaven
    With the sun's cloudless orb,
    Whose rays of rapid light
Parted around the chariot's swifter course,
And fell like ocean's feathery spray
    Dashed from the boiling surge
    Before a vessel's prow.

THE DÆMON OF THE WORLD.

The magic car moved on.
Earth's distant orb appeared
The smallest light that twinkles in the heavens,
 Whilst round the chariot's way
Innumerable systems widely rolled,
 And countless spheres diffused
  An ever varying glory.
It was a sight of wonder! Some were horned,
And, like the moon's argentine crescent hung
In the dark dome of heaven, some did shed
A clear mild beam like Hesperus, while the sea
Yet glows with fading sun-light; others dashed
Athwart the night with trains of bickering fire,
Like spherèd worlds to death and ruin driven;
Some shone like stars, and as the chariot passed
 Bedimmed all other light.

 Spirit of Nature! here
In this interminable wilderness
Of worlds, at whose involved immensity
 Even soaring fancy staggers,
 Here is thy fitting temple.
 Yet not the lightest leaf
That quivers to the passing breeze
 Is less instinct with thee,—
 Yet not the meanest worm,

THE DÆMON OF THE WORLD.

That lurks in graves and fattens on the dead
    Less shares thy eternal breath.
    Spirit of Nature ! thou
Imperishable as this glorious scene,
    Here is thy fitting temple.

If solitude hath ever led thy steps
To the shore of the immeasurable sea,
    And thou hast lingered there
    Until the sun's broad orb
Seemed resting on the fiery line of ocean,
Thou must have marked the braided webs of gold
    That without motion hang
    Over the sinking sphere :
Thou must have marked the billowy mountain clouds,
Edged with intolerable radiancy,
    Towering like rocks of jet
    Above the burning deep :
    And yet there is a moment
    When the sun's highest point
Peers like a star o'er ocean's western edge,
When those far clouds of feathery purple gleam
Like fairy lands girt by some heavenly sea :
Then has thy rapt imagination soared
Where in the midst of all existing things
The temple of the mightiest Dæmon stands.

  Yet not the golden islands
That gleam amid yon flood of purple light,
  Nor the feathery curtains
That canopy the sun's resplendent couch,
  Nor the burnished ocean waves
  Paving that gorgeous dome,
  So fair, so wonderful a sight
As the eternal temple could afford.
The elements of all that human thought
Can frame of lovely or sublime, did join
To rear the fabric of the fane, nor aught
Of earth may image forth its majesty.
Yet likest evening's vault that faëry hall,
As heaven low resting on the wave it spread
  Its floors of flashing light,
  Its vast and azure dome;
And on the verge of that obscure abyss
Where crystal battlements o'erhang the gulph
Of the dark world, ten thousand spheres diffuse
Their lustre through its adamantine gates.

  The magic car no longer moved;
  The Dæmon and the Spirit
  Entered the eternal gates.
  Those clouds of aery gold
  That slept in glittering billows

THE DÆMON OF THE WORLD.

Beneath the azure canopy,
With the etherial footsteps trembled not;
While slight and odorous mists
Floated to strains of thrilling melody
Through the vast columns and the pearly shrines.

The Dæmon and the Spirit
Approached the overhanging battlement.
Below lay stretched the boundless universe!
There, far as the remotest line
That limits swift imagination's flight,
Unending orbs mingled in mazy motion,
Immutably fulfilling
Eternal Nature's law.
Above, below, around,
The circling systems formed
A wilderness of harmony,
Each with undeviating aim
In eloquent silence through the depths of space
Pursued its wondrous way.—

Awhile the Spirit paused in ecstasy.
Yet soon she saw, as the vast spheres swept by,
Strange things within their belted orbs appear.
Like animated frenzies, dimly moved
Shadows, and skeletons, and fiendly shapes,

THE DÆMON OF THE WORLD.

Thronging round human graves, and o'er the dead
Sculpturing records for each memory
In verse, such as malignant gods pronounce,
Blasting the hopes of men, when heaven and hell
Confounded burst in ruin o'er the world:
And they did build vast trophies, instruments
Of murder, human bones, barbaric gold,
Skins torn from living men, and towers of skulls
With sightless holes gazing on blinder heaven,
Mitres, and crowns, and brazen chariots stained
With blood, and scrolls of mystic wickedness,
The sanguine codes of venerable crime.
The likeness of a thronèd king came by,
When these had past, bearing upon his brow
A threefold crown; his countenance was calm,
His eye severe and cold; but his right hand
Was charged with bloody coin, and he did gnaw
By fits, with secret smiles, a human heart
Concealed beneath his robe; and motley shapes,
A multitudinous throng, around him knelt,
With bosoms bare, and bowed heads, and false looks
Of true submission, as the sphere rolled by,
Brooking no eye to witness their foul shame,
Which human hearts must feel, while human tongues
Tremble to speak, they did rage horribly,
Breathing in self contempt fierce blasphemies

Against the Dæmon of the World, and high
Hurling their armèd hands where the pure Spirit,
Serene and inaccessibly secure,
Stood on an isolated pinnacle,
The flood of ages combating below
The depth of the unbounded universe
    Above, and all around
Necessity's unchanging harmony.

SECOND PART.

O HAPPY Earth! reality of Heaven!
To which those restless powers that ceaselessly
Throng through the human universe, aspire;
Thou consummation of all mortal hope!
Thou glorious prize of blindly-working will!
Whose rays, diffused throughout all space and time,
Verge to one point and blend forever there:
Of purest spirits thou pure dwelling-place!
Where care and sorrow, impotence and crime,
Languor, disease, and ignorance dare not come:
O happy Earth, reality of Heaven!

  Genius has seen thee in her passionate dreams,
And dim forebodings of thy loveliness

THE DÆMON OF THE WORLD.

Haunting the human heart, have there entwined
Those rooted hopes, that the proud Power of Evil
Shall not forever on this fairest world
Shake pestilence and war, or that his slaves
With blasphemy for prayer, and human blood
For sacrifice, before his shrine forever
In adoration bend, or Erebus
With all its banded fiends shall not uprise
To overwhelm in envy and revenge
The dauntless and the good, who dare to hurl
Defiance at his throne, girt tho' it be
With Death's omnipotence. Thou hast beheld
His empire, o'er the present and the past;
It was a desolate sight — now gaze on mine,
Futurity. Thou hoary giant Time,
Render thou up thy half-devoured babes, —
And from the cradles of eternity,
Where millions lie lulled to their portioned sleep
By the deep murmuring stream of passing things,
Tear thou that gloomy shroud. — Spirit, behold
Thy glorious destiny!

      The Spirit saw
The vast frame of the renovated world
Smile in the lap of Chaos, and the sense
Of hope thro' her fine texture did suffuse

Such varying glow, as summer evening casts
On undulating clouds and deepening lakes.
Like the vague sighings of a wind at even,
That wakes the wavelets of the slumbering sea
And dies on the creation of its breath,
And sinks and rises, fails and swells by fits:
Was the sweet stream of thought that with mild motion
Flowed o'er the Spirit's human sympathies.
The mighty tide of thought had paused awhile,
Which from the Dæmon now like Ocean's stream
Again began to pour.—

     To me is given
The wonders of the human world to keep—
Space, matter, time and mind—let the sight
Renew and strengthen all thy failing hope.
All things are recreated, and the flame
Of consentaneous love inspires all life:
The fertile bosom of the earth gives suck
To myriads, who still grow beneath her care,
Rewarding her with their pure perfectness:
The balmy breathings of the wind inhale
Her virtues, and diffuse them all abroad:
Health floats amid the gentle atmosphere,
Glows in the fruits, and mantles on the stream:
No storms deform the beaming brow of heaven,

Nor scatter in the freshness of its pride
The foliage of the undecaying trees;
But fruits are ever ripe, flowers ever fair,
And Autumn proudly bears her matron grace,
Kindling a flush on the fair cheek of Spring,
Whose virgin bloom beneath the ruddy fruit
Reflects its tint and blushes into love.

The habitable earth is full of bliss;
Those wastes of frozen billows that were hurled
By everlasting snow-storms round the poles,
Where matter dared nor vegetate nor live,
But ceaseless frost round the vast solitude
Bound its broad zone of stillness, are unloosed;
And fragrant zephyrs there from spicy isles
Ruffle the placid ocean-deep, that rolls
Its broad, bright surges to the sloping sand,
Whose roar is wakened into echoings sweet
To murmur through the heaven-breathing groves
And melodize with man's blest nature there.

The vast tract of the parched and sandy waste
Now teems with countless rills and shady woods,
Corn-fields and pastures and white cottages;
And where the startled wilderness did hear
A savage conqueror stained in kindred blood,

Hymning his victory, or the milder snake
Crushing the bones of some frail antelope
Within his brazen folds — the dewy lawn,
Offering sweet incense to the sun-rise, smiles
To see a babe before his mother's door,
Share with the green and golden basilisk
That comes to lick his feet, his morning's meal.

   Those trackless deeps, where many a weary sail
Has seen above the illimitable plain,
Morning on night, and night on morning rise,
Whilst still no land to greet the wanderer spread
Its shadowy mountains on the sun-bright sea,
Where the loud roarings of the tempest-waves
So long have mingled with the gusty wind
In melancholy loneliness, and swept
The desert of those ocean solitudes,
But vocal to the sea-bird's harrowing shriek,
The bellowing monster, and the rushing storm,
Now to the sweet and many mingling sounds
Of kindliest human impulses respond:
Those lonely realms bright garden-isles begem,
With lightsome clouds and shining seas between,
And fertile vallies, resonant with bliss,
Whilst green woods overcanopy the wave,

Which like a toil-worn labourer leaps to shore,
To meet the kisses of the flowrets there.

    Man chief perceives the change, his being notes
The gradual renovation, and defines
Each movement of its progress on his mind.
Man, where the gloom of the long polar night
Lowered o'er the snow-clad rocks and frozen soil,
Where scarce the hardest herb that braves the frost
Basked in the moonlight's ineffectual glow,
Shrank with the plants, and darkened with the night;
Nor where the tropics bound the realms of day
With a broad belt of mingling cloud and flame,
Where blue mists through the unmoving atmosphere
Scattered the seeds of pestilence, and fed
Unnatural vegetation, where the land
Teemed with all earthquake, tempest and disease,
Was man a nobler being; slavery
Had crushed him to his country's bloodstained dust.

    Even where the milder zone afforded man
A seeming shelter, yet contagion there,
Blighting his being with unnumbered ills,
Spread like a quenchless fire; nor truth availed
Till late to arrest its progress, or create
That peace which first in bloodless victory waved

Her snowy standard o'er this favoured clime:
There man was long the train-bearer of slaves,
The mimic of surrounding misery,
The jackal of ambition's lion-rage,
The bloodhound of religion's hungry zeal.

  Here now the human being stands adorning
This loveliest earth with taintless body and mind;
Blest from his birth with all bland impulses,
Which gently in his noble bosom wake
All kindly passions and all pure desires.
Him, still from hope to hope the bliss pursuing,
Which from the exhaustless lore of human weal
Draws on the virtuous mind, the thoughts that rise
In time-destroying infiniteness, gift
With self-enshrined eternity, that mocks
The unprevailing hoariness of age,
And man, once fleeting o'er the transient scene.
Swift as an unremembered vision, stands
Immortal upon earth: no longer now
He slays the beast that sports around his dwelling
And horribly devours its mangled flesh,
Or drinks its vital blood, which like a stream
Of poison thro' his fevered veins did flow
Feeding a plague that secretly consumed
His feeble frame, and kindling in his mind

Hatred, despair, and fear and vain belief,
The germs of misery, death, disease, and crime.
No longer now the wingèd habitants,
That in the woods their sweet lives sing away,
Flee from the form of man; but gather round,
And prune their sunny feathers on the hands
Which little children stretch in friendly sport
Towards these dreadless partners of their play.
All things are void of terror: man has lost
His desolating privilege, and stands
An equal amidst equals: happiness
And science dawn though late upon the earth;
Peace cheers the mind, health renovates the frame;
Disease and pleasure cease to mingle here,
Reason and passion cease to combat there;
Whilst mind unfettered o'er the earth extends
Its all-subduing energies, and wields
The sceptre of a vast dominion there.

Mild is the slow necessity of death:
The tranquil spirit fails beneath its grasp,
Without a groan, almost without a fear,
Resigned in peace to the necessity,
Calm as a voyager to some distant land,
And full of wonder, full of hope as he.
The deadly germs of languor and disease

THE DÆMON OF THE WORLD.

Waste in the human frame, and Nature gifts
With choicest boons her human worshippers.
How vigorous now the athletic form of age !
How clear its open and unwrinkled brow !
Where neither avarice, cunning, pride, or care,
Had stamped the seal of grey deformity
On all the mingling lineaments of time.
How lovely the intrepid front of youth !
How sweet the smiles of taintless infancy.

Within the massy prison's mouldering courts,
Fearless and free the ruddy children play,
Weaving gay chaplets for their innocent brows
With the green ivy and the red wall-flower,
That mock the dungeon's unavailing gloom ;
The ponderous chains, and gratings of strong iron,
There rust amid the accumulated ruins
Now mingling slowly with their native earth :
There the broad beam of day, which feebly once
Lighted the cheek of lean captivity
With a pale and sickly glare, now freely shines
On the pure smiles of infant playfulness :
No more the shuddering voice of hoarse despair
Peals through the echoing vaults, but soothing notes
Of ivy-fingered winds and gladsome birds
And merriment are resonant around.

THE DÆMON OF THE WORLD.

The fanes of Fear and Falsehood hear no more
The voice that once waked multitudes to war
Thundering thro' all their aisles : but now respond
To the death dirge of the melancholy wind :
It were a sight of awfulness to see
The works of faith and slavery, so vast,
So sumptuous, yet withal so perishing !
Even as the corpse that rests beneath their wall.
A thousand mourners deck the pomp of death
To-day, the breathing marble glows above
To decorate its memory, and tongues
Are busy of its life : to-morrow, worms
In silence and in darkness seize their prey.
These ruins soon leave not a wreck behind :
Their elements, wide scattered o'er the globe,
To happier shapes are moulded, and become
Ministrant to all blissful impulses :
Thus human things are perfected, and earth,
Even as a child beneath its mother's love,
Is strengthened in all excellence, and grows
Fairer and nobler with each passing year.

Now Time his dusky pennons o'er the scene
Closes in steadfast darkness, and the past
Fades from our charmèd sight. My task is done :
Thy lore is learned. Earth's wonders are thine own,

THE DÆMON OF THE WORLD.

With all the fear and all the hope they bring.
My spells are past: the present now recurs.
Ah me! a pathless wilderness remains
Yet unsubdued by man's reclaiming hand.

  Yet, human Spirit, bravely hold thy course,
Let virtue teach thee firmly to pursue
The gradual paths of an aspiring change:
For birth and life and death, and that strange state
Before the naked powers that thro' the world
Wander like winds have found a human home,
All tend to perfect happiness, and urge
The restless wheels of being on their way,
Whose flashing spokes, instinct with infinite life,
Bicker and burn to gain their destined goal:
For birth but wakes the universal mind
Whose mighty streams might else in silence flow
Thro' the vast world, to individual sense
Of outward shews, whose unexperienced shape
New modes of passion to its frame may lend;
Life is its state of action, and the store
Of all events is aggregated there
That variegate the eternal universe;
Death is a gate of dreariness and gloom,
That leads to azure isles and beaming skies
And happy regions of eternal hope.

Therefore, O Spirit! fearlessly bear on:
Though storms may break the primrose on its stalk,
Though frosts may blight the freshness of its bloom,
Yet spring's awakening breath will woo the earth,
To feed with kindliest dews its favorite flower,
That blooms in mossy banks and darksome glens,
Lighting the green wood with its sunny smile.

Fear not then, Spirit, death's disrobing hand,
So welcome when the tyrant is awake,
So welcome when the bigot's hell-torch flares;
'Tis but the voyage of a darksome hour,
The transient gulph-dream of a startling sleep.
For what thou art shall perish utterly,
But what is thine may never cease to be;
Death is no foe to virtue: earth has seen
Love's brightest roses on the scaffold bloom,
Mingling with freedom's fadeless laurels there,
And presaging the truth of visioned bliss.
Are there not hopes within thee, which this scene
Of linked and gradual being has confirmed?
Hopes that not vainly thou, and living fires
Of mind, as radiant and as pure as thou
Have shone upon the paths of men — return
Surpassing Spirit, to that world, where thou
Art destined an eternal war to wage

THE DÆMON OF THE WORLD.

With tyranny and falsehood, and uproot
The germs of misery from the human heart.
Thine is the hand whose piety would soothe
The thorny pillow of unhappy crime,
Whose impotence an easy pardon gains,
Watching its wanderings as a friend's disease:
Thine is the brow whose mildness would defy
Its fiercest rage, and brave its sternest will,
When fenced by power and master of the world.
Thou art sincere and good; of resolute mind,
Free from heart-withering custom's cold control,
Of passion lofty, pure and unsubdued.
Earth's pride and meanness could not vanquish thee,
And therefore art thou worthy of the boon
Which thou hast now received: virtue shall keep
Thy footsteps in the path that thou hast trod,
And many days of beaming hope shall bless
Thy spotless life of sweet and sacred love.
Go, happy one, and give that bosom joy
  Whose sleepless spirit waits to catch
  Light, life and rapture from thy smile.

The Dæmon called its wingèd ministers.
Speechless with bliss the Spirit mounts the car,
That rolled beside the crystal battlement,
Bending her beamy eyes in thankfulness.

> The burning wheels inflame
> The steep descent of Heaven's untrodden way.
>   Fast and far the chariot flew:
>   The mighty globes that rolled
> Around the gate of the Eternal Fane
> Lessened by slow degrees, and soon appeared
> Such tiny twinklers as the planet orbs
> That ministering on the solar power
> With borrowed light pursued their narrower way.
>   Earth floated then below:
>   The chariot paused a moment;
>   The Spirit then descended:
>   And from the earth departing
>   The shadows with swift wings
> Speeded like thought upon the light of Heaven.
>
>   The Body and the Soul united then,
> A gentle start convulsed Ianthe's frame:
> Her veiny eyelids quietly unclosed;
> Moveless awhile the dark blue orbs remained:
> She looked around in wonder and beheld
> Henry, who kneeled in silence by her couch,
> Watching her sleep with looks of speechless love,
>   And the bright beaming stars
>   That through the casement shone.

TO MARY WOLLSTONECRAFT GODWIN.

I.

Mine eyes were dim with tears unshed;
   Yes, I was firm — thus wert not thou;—
My baffled looks did fear yet dread
   To meet thy looks — I could not know
How anxiously they sought to shine
With soothing pity upon mine.

II.

To sit and curb the soul's mute rage
   Which preys upon itself alone;
To curse the life which is the cage
   Of fettered grief that dares not groan,
Hiding from many a careless eye
The scornèd load of agony.

III.

Whilst thou alone, then not regarded,
   The   thou alone should be,
To spend years thus, and be rewarded,
   As thou, sweet love, requited me
When none were near — Oh! I did wake
From torture for that moment's sake.

LINES TO MARY WOLLSTONECRAFT GODWIN.

IV.

Upon my heart thy accents sweet
   Of peace and pity fell like dew
On flowers half dead;— thy lips did meet
   Mine tremblingly; thy dark eyes threw
Their soft persuasion on my brain,
Charming away its dream of pain.

V.

We are not happy, sweet! our state
   Is strange and full of doubt and fear;
More need of words that ills abate;—
   Reserve or censure come not near
Our sacred friendship, lest there be
No solace left for thee and me.

VI.

Gentle and good and mild thou art,
   Nor can I live if thou appear
Aught but thyself, or turn thine heart
   Away from me, or stoop to wear
The mask of scorn, although it be
To hide the love thou 'feel'st for me.

LINES.

I.

The cold earth slept below;
  Above the cold sky shone;
    And all around,
    With a chilling sound,
From caves of ice and fields of snow,
The breath of night like death did flow
  Beneath the sinking moon.

II.

The wintry hedge was black,
  The green grass was not seen,
    The birds did rest
    On the bare thorn's breast,
Whose roots, beside the pathway track,
Had bound their folds o'er many a crack
  Which the frost had made between.

III.

Thine eyes glowed in the glare
  Of the moon's dying light;
    As a fen-fire's beam,
    On a sluggish stream,
Gleams dimly — so the moon shone there,
And it yellowed the strings of thy tangled hair
  That shook in the wind of night.

"YET LOOK ON ME."

IV.

The moon made thy lips pale, beloved;
　The wind made thy bosom chill;
　　The night did shed
　　On thy dear head
Its frozen dew, and thou didst lie
Where the bitter breath of the naked sky
　Might visit thee at will.

TO ———.

Yet look on me — take not thine eyes away,
　Which feed upon the love within mine own,
Which is indeed but the reflected ray
　Of thine own beauty from my spirit thrown.
　Yet speak to me — thy voice is as the tone
Of my heart's echo, and I think I hear
　That thou yet lovest me; yet thou alone
Like one before a mirror, without care
Of aught but thine own features, imaged there;
And yet I wear out life in watching thee;
　A toil so sweet at times, and thou indeed
Art kind when I am sick, and pity me.

MONT BLANC.

LINES WRITTEN IN THE VALE OF CHAMOUNI.

I.

THE everlasting universe of things
Flows through the mind, and rolls its rapid waves,
Now dark — now glittering — now reflecting gloom —
Now lending splendour, where from secret springs
The source of human thought its tribute brings
Of waters, — with a sound but half its own,
Such as a feeble brook will oft assume
In the wild woods, among the mountains lone,
Where waterfalls around it leap for ever,
Where woods and winds contend, and a vast river
Over its rocks ceaselessly bursts and raves.

II.

Thus thou, Ravine of Arve — dark, deep Ravine —
Thou many-coloured, many-voicèd vale,
Over whose pines, and crags, and caverns sail
Fast cloud shadows and sunbeams : awful scene,

Where Power in likeness of the Arve comes down
From the ice gulphs that gird his secret throne,
Bursting through these dark mountains like the flame
Of lightning thro' the tempest;—thou dost lie,
Thy giant brood of pines around thee clinging,
Children of elder time, in whose devotion
The chainless winds still come and ever came
To drink their odours, and their mighty swinging
To hear—an old and solemn harmony;
Thine earthly rainbows stretched across the sweep
Of the ethereal waterfall, whose veil
Robes some unsculptured image; the strange sleep
Which when the voices of the desart fail
Wraps all in its own deep eternity;—
Thy caverns echoing to the Arve's commotion,
A loud, lone sound no other sound can tame;
Thou art pervaded with that ceaseless motion,
Thou art the path of that unresting sound—
Dizzy Ravine! and when I gaze on thee
I seem as in a trance sublime and strange
To muse on my own separate phantasy,
My own, my human mind, which passively
Now renders and receives fast influencings,
Holding an unremitting interchange
With the clear universe of things around;
One legion of wild thoughts, whose wandering wings

Now float above thy darkness, and now rest
Where that or thou art no unbidden guest,
In the still cave of the witch Poesy,
Seeking among the shadows that pass by
Ghosts of all things that are, some shade of thee,
Some phantom, some faint image ; till the breast
From which they fled recalls them, thou art there !

III.

Some say that gleams of a remoter world
Visit the soul in sleep, — that death is slumber,
And that its shapes the busy thoughts outnumber
Of those who wake and live. — I look on high ;
Has some unknown omnipotence unfurled
The veil of life and death? or do I lie
In dream, and does the mightier world of sleep
Spread far around and inaccessibly
Its circles? For the very spirit fails,
Driven like a homeless cloud from steep to steep
That vanishes among the viewless gales !
Far, far above, piercing the infinite sky,
Mont Blanc appears, — still, snowy, and serene —
Its subject mountains their unearthly forms
Pile around it, ice and rock ; broad vales between
Of frozen floods, unfathomable deeps,
Blue as the overhanging heaven, that spread

And wind among the accumulated steeps;
A desart peopled by the storms alone,
Save when the eagle brings some hunter's bone,
And the wolf tracks her there — how hideously
Its shapes are heaped around! rude, bare, and high,
Ghastly, and scarred, and riven. — Is this the scene
Where the old Earthquake-dæmon taught her young
Ruin? Were these their toys? or did a sea
Of fire, envelope once this silent snow?
None can reply — all seems eternal now.
The wilderness has a mysterious tongue
Which teaches awful doubt, or faith so mild,
So solemn, so serene, that man may be
But for such faith with nature reconciled;
Thou hast a voice, great Mountain, to repeal
Large codes of fraud and woe; not understood
By all, but which the wise, and great, and good
Interpret, or make felt, or deeply feel.

IV.

The fields, the lakes, the forests, and the streams,
Ocean, and all the living things that dwell
Within the dædal earth; lightning, and rain,
Earthquake, and fiery flood, and hurricane,
The torpor of the year when feeble dreams
Visit the hidden buds, or dreamless sleep

Holds every future leaf and flower;—the bound
With which from that detested trance they leap;
The works and ways of man, their death and birth,
And that of him and all that his may be;
All things that move and breathe with toil and sound
Are born and die; revolve, subside and swell.
Power dwells apart in its tranquillity
Remote, serene, and inaccessible:
And *this*, the naked countenance of earth,
On which I gaze, even these primæval mountains
Teach the adverting mind. The glaciers creep
Like snakes that watch their prey, from their far fountains,
Slow rolling on; there, many a precipice,
Frost and the Sun in scorn of mortal power
Have piled: dome, pyramid, and pinnacle,
A city of death, distinct with many a tower
And wall impregnable of beaming ice.
Yet not a city, but a flood of ruin
Is there, that from the boundaries of the sky
Rolls its perpetual stream; vast pines are strewing
Its destined path, or in the mangled soil
Branchless and shattered stand; the rocks, drawn down
From yon remotest waste, have overthrown
The limits of the dead and living world,
Never to be reclaimed. The dwelling-place
Of insects, beasts, and birds, becomes its spoil;

Their food and their retreat for ever gone,
So much of life and joy is lost.   The race
Of man, flies far in dread; his work and dwelling
Vanish, like smoke before the tempest's stream,
And their place is not known.   Below, vast caves
Shine in the rushing torrent's restless gleam,
Which from those secret chasms in tumult welling
Meet in the vale, and one majestic River,
The breath and blood of distant lands, for ever
Rolls its loud waters to the ocean waves,
Breathes its swift vapours to the circling air.

v.

Mont Blanc yet gleams on high :— the power is there,
The still and solemn power of many sights,
And many sounds, and much of life and death.
In the calm darkness of the moonless nights,
In the lone glare of day, the snows descend
Upon that Mountain; none beholds them there,
Nor when the flakes burn in the sinking sun,
Or the star-beams dart through them :— Winds contend
Silently there, and heap the snow with breath
Rapid and strong, but silently!   Its home
The voiceless lightning in these solitudes
Keeps innocently, and like vapour broods
Over the snow.   The secret strength of things

ich governs thought, and to the infinite dome
heaven is as a law, inhabits thee!
d what were thou, and earth, and stars, and sea,
to the human mind's imaginings
ence and solitude were vacancy?

―――――

ON FANNY GODWIN.

HER voice did quiver as we parted,
   Yet knew I not that heart was broken
From which it came, and I departed
   Heeding not the words then spoken.
     Misery — O Misery,
     This world is all too wide for thee.

HYMN TO INTELLECTUAL BEAUTY.

1.

The awful shadow of some unseen Power
    Floats tho' unseen amongst us,—visiting
    This various world with as inconstant wing
As summer winds that creep from flower to flower,-
Like moonbeams that behind some piny mount
        shower,
    It visits with inconstant glance
    Each human heart and countenance;
Like hues and harmonies of evening,—
    Like clouds in starlight widely spread,—
    Like memory of music fled,—
    Like aught that for its grace may be
Dear, and yet dearer for its mystery.

2.

Spirit of BEAUTY, that dost consecrate
    With thine own hues all thou dost shine upon
    Of human thought or form,—where art thou go
Why dost thou pass away and leave our state,
This dim vast vale of tears, vacant and desolate?

Ask why the sunlight not for ever
Weaves rainbows o'er yon mountain river,
Why aught should fail and fade that once is shewn,
Why fear and dream and death and birth
Cast on the daylight of this earth
Such gloom,—why man has such a scope
For love and hate, despondency and hope?

3.

No voice from some sublimer world hath ever
To sage or poet these responses given—
Therefore the names of Demon, Ghost, and Heaven,
Remain the records of their vain endeavour,
Frail spells—whose uttered charm might not avail to sever,
From all we hear and all we see,
Doubt, chance, and mutability.
Thy light alone—like mist o'er mountains driven,
Or music by the night wind sent,
Thro' strings of some still instrument,
Or moonlight on a midnight stream,
Gives grace and truth to life's unquiet dream.

4.

Love, Hope, and Self-esteem, like clouds depart
And come, for some uncertain moments lent.

Man were immortal, and omnipotent,
Didst thou, unknown and awful as thou art,
Keep with thy glorious train firm state within his h
    Thou messenger of sympathies,
     That wax and wane in lovers' eyes —
Thou — that to human thought art nourishment,
     Like darkness to a dying flame !
     Depart not as thy shadow came,
     Depart not — lest the grave should be,
Like life and fear, a dark reality.

5.

While yet a boy I sought for ghosts, and sped
   Thro' many a listening chamber, cave and ruin,
   And starlight wood, with fearful steps pursuing
Hopes of high talk with the departed dead.
I called on poisonous names with which our youth is
     I was not heard — I saw them not —
     When musing deeply on the lot
Of life, at that sweet time when winds are wooing
     All vital things that wake to bring
     News of birds and blossoming, —
     Sudden, thy shadow fell on me ;
I shrieked, and clasped my hands in ecstasy !

6.

I vowed that I would dedicate my powers
   To thee and thine — have I not kept the vow?

With beating heart and streaming eyes, even now
I call the phantoms of a thousand hours
Each from his voiceless grave: they have in visioned
   bowers
   Of studious zeal or love's delight
   Outwatched with me the envious night—
They know that never joy illumed my brow
   Unlinked with hope that thou wouldst free
   This world from its dark slavery,
   That thou—O awful LOVELINESS,
Wouldst give whate'er these words cannot express.

7.

The day becomes more solemn and serene
   When noon is past—there is a harmony
   In autumn, and a lustre in its sky,
Which thro' the summer is not heard or seen,
As if it could not be, as if it had not been!
   Thus let thy power, which like the truth
   Of nature on my passive youth
Descended, to my onward life supply
   Its calm—to one who worships thee,
   And every form containing thee,
   Whom, SPIRIT fair, thy spells did bind
To fear himself, and love all human kind.

THE SUNSET.

THERE late was One within whose subtle being,
As light and wind within some delicate cloud
That fades amid the blue noon's burning sky,—
Genius and death contended. None may know
The sweetness of the joy which made his breath
Fail, like the trances of the summer air,
When, with the Lady of his love, who then
First knew the unreserve of mingled being,
He walked along the pathway of a field
Which to the east a hoar wood shadowed o'er,
But to the west was open to the sky.
There now the sun had sunk, but lines of gold
Hung on the ashen clouds, and on the points
Of the far level grass and nodding flowers
And the old dandelion's hoary beard,
And, mingled with the shades of twilight, lay
On the brown massy woods — and in the east
The broad and burning moon lingeringly rose
Between the black trunks of the crowded trees,
While the faint stars were gathering overhead. —
"Is it not strange, Isabel," said the youth,

THE SUNSET.

"I never saw the sun-rise? We will wake here
To-morrow; thou shalt look on it with me."

    That night the youth and lady mingled lay
In love and sleep — but when the morning came
The lady found her lover dead and cold.
Let none believe that God in mercy gave
That stroke. The lady died not, nor grew wild,
But year by year lived on — in truth I think
Her gentleness and patience and sad smiles,
And that she did not die, but lived to tend
Her agèd father, were a kind of madness,
If madness 'tis to be unlike the world.
For but to see her were to read the tale
Woven by some subtlest bard, to make hard hearts
Dissolve away in wisdom-working grief; —
Her eyelashes were worn away with tears,
Her lips and cheeks were like things dead — so pale;
Her hands were thin, and through their wandering veins
And weak articulations might be seen
Day's ruddy light. The tomb of thy dead self
Which one vexed ghost inhabits, night and day,
Is all, lost child, that now remains of thee!

    "Inheritor of more than earth can give,
Passionless calm and silence unreproved,

Whether the dead find, oh, not sleep! but rest,
And are the uncomplaining things they seem,
Or live, or drop in the deep sea of Love;
Oh, that like thine, mine epitaph were — Peace!"
This was the only moan she ever made.

MARIANNE'S DREAM.

I.

A PALE dream came to a Lady fair,
   And said, A boon, a boon, I pray!
I know the secrets of the air,
   And things are lost in the glare of day,
Which I can make the sleeping see,
If they will put their trust in me.

II.

And thou shalt know of things unknown,
   If thou wilt let me rest between
The veiny lids, whose fringe is thrown
   Over thine eyes so dark and sheen:
And half in hope, and half in fright,
The Lady closed her eyes so bright.

III.

At first all deadly shapes were driven
    Tumultuously across her sleep,
And o'er the vast cope of bending heaven
    All ghastly-visaged clouds did sweep;
And the Lady ever looked to spy
If the golden sun shone forth on high.

IV.

And as towards the east she turned,
    She saw aloft in the morning air,
Which now with hues of sunrise burned,
    A great black Anchor rising there;
And wherever the Lady turned her eyes,
It hung before her in the skies.

V.

The sky was blue as the summer sea,
    The depths were cloudless over head,
The air was calm as it could be,
    There was no sight or sound of dread,
But that black Anchor floating still
Over the piny eastern hill.

VI.

The Lady grew sick with a weight of fear,
    To see that Anchor ever hanging,
And veiled her eyes; she then did hear
    The sound as of a dim low clanging,
And looked abroad if she might know
Was it aught else, or but the flow
Of the blood in her own veins, to and fro.

VII.

There was a mist in the sunless air,
    Which shook as it were with an earthquake's shock,
But the very weeds that blossomed there
    Were moveless, and each mighty rock
Stood on its basis steadfastly;
The Anchor was seen no more on high.

VIII.

But piled around, with summits hid
    In lines of cloud at intervals,
Stood many a mountain pyramid
    Among whose everlasting walls
Two mighty cities shone, and ever
Through the red mist their domes did quiver.

IX.

On two dread mountains, from whose crest,
    Might seem, the eagle, for her brood,
Would ne'er have hung her dizzy nest,
    Those tower-encircled cities stood.
A vision strange such towers to see,
Sculptured and wrought so gorgeously,
Where human art could never be.

X.

And columns framed of marble white,
    And giant fanes, dome over dome
Piled, and triumphant gates, all bright
    With workmanship, which could not come
From touch of mortal instrument,
Shot o'er the vales, or lustre lent
From its own shapes magnificent.

XI.

But still the Lady heard that clang
    Filling the wide air far away;
And still the mist whose light did hang
    Among the mountains shook alway,
So that the Lady's heart beat fast,
As half in joy, and half aghast,
On those high domes her look she cast.

XII.

Sudden, from out that city sprung
   A light that made the earth grow red;
Two flames that each with quivering tongue
   Licked its high domes, and over head
Among those mighty towers and fanes
Dropped fire, as a volcano rains
Its sulphurous ruin on the plains.

XIII.

And hark! a rush as if the deep
   Had burst its bonds; she looked behind
And saw over the western steep
   A raging flood descend, and wind
Through that wide vale; she felt no fear,
But said within herself, 'Tis clear
These towers are Nature's own, and she
To save them has sent forth the sea.

XIV.

And now those raging billows came
   Where that fair Lady sate, and she
Was borne towards the showering flame
   By the wild waves heaped tumultuously,
And on a little plank, the flow
Of the whirlpool bore her to and fro.

XV.

The flames were fiercely vomited
   From every tower and every dome,
And dreary light did widely shed
   O'er that vast flood's suspended foam,
Beneath the smoke which hung its night
On the stained cope of heaven's light.

XVI.

The plank whereon that Lady sate
   Was driven through the chasms, about and about,
Between the peaks so desolate
   Of the drowning mountains, in and out,
As the thistle-beard on a whirlwind sails —
While the flood was filling those hollow vales.

XVII.

At last her plank an eddy crost,
   And bore her to the city's wall,
Which now the flood had reached almost;
   It might the stoutest heart appal
To hear the fire roar and hiss
Through the domes of those mighty palaces.

XVIII.

The eddy whirled her round and round
  Before a gorgeous gate, which stood
Piercing the clouds of smoke which bound
  Its aëry arch with light like blood;
She looked on that gate of marble clear,
With wonder that extinguished fear.

XIX.

For it was filled with sculptures rarest,
  Of forms most beautiful and strange,
Like nothing human, but the fairest
  Of wingèd shapes, whose legions range
Throughout the sleep of those that are,
Like this same Lady, good and fair.

XX.

And as she looked, still lovelier grew
  Those marble forms;—the sculptor sure
Was a strong spirit, and the hue
  Of his own mind did there endure
After the touch, whose power had braided
Such grace, was in some sad change faded.

XXI.

She looked, the flames were dim, the flood
   Grew tranquil as a woodland river
Winding through hills in solitude;
   Those marble shapes then seemed to quiver,
And their fair limbs to float in motion,
Like weeds unfolding in the ocean.

XXII.

And their lips moved; one seemed to speak,
   When suddenly the mountain crackt,
And through the chasm the flood did break
   With an earth-uplifting cataract:
The statues gave a joyous scream,
And on its wings the pale thin dream
Lifted the Lady from the stream.

XXIII.

The dizzy flight of that phantom pale
   Waked the fair Lady from her sleep,
And she arose, while from the veil
   Of her dark eyes the dream did creep,
And she walked about as one who knew
That sleep has sights as clear and true
As any waking eyes can view.

TO CONSTANTIA,

SINGING.

I.

Thus to be lost and thus to sink and die,
   Perchance were death indeed!—Constantia, turn!
In thy dark eyes a power like light doth lie,
   Even though the sounds which were thy voice, which
      burn
Between thy lips, are laid to sleep;
   Within thy breath, and on thy hair, like odour it is
      yet,
And from thy touch like fire doth leap.
   Even while I write, my burning cheeks are wet,
   Alas, that the torn heart can bleed, but not forget!

II.

A breathless awe, like the swift change
   Unseen, but felt in youthful slumbers,
Wild, sweet, but uncommunicably strange,
   Thou breathest now in fast ascending numbers.
The cope of heaven seems rent and cloven
   By the inchantment of thy strain,
And on my shoulders wings are woven,
   To follow its sublime career,

TO CONSTANTIA.

Beyond the mighty moons that wane
   Upon the verge of nature's utmost sphere,
   Till the world's shadowy walls are past and disappear.

III.

Her voice is hovering o'er my soul — it lingers
   O'ershadowing it with soft and lulling wings,
The blood and life within those snowy fingers
   Teach witchcraft to the instrumental strings.
My brain is wild, my breath comes quick —
   The blood is listening in my frame,
And thronging shadows, fast and thick,
   Fall on my overflowing eyes;
My heart is quivering like a flame;
   As morning dew, that in the sunbeam dies,
   I am dissolved in these consuming ecstasies.

IV.

I have no life, Constantia, now, but thee,
   Whilst, like the world-surrounding air, thy song
Flows on, and fills all things with melody. —
   Now is thy voice a tempest swift and strong,
On which, like one in trance upborne,
   Secure o'er rocks and waves I sweep,
Rejoicing like a cloud of morn.

Now 'tis the breath of summer night,
Which when the starry waters sleep,
  Round western isles, with incense-blossoms bright,
Lingering, suspends my soul in its voluptuous flight.

TO CONSTANTIA.

I.

THE rose that drinks the fountain dew
  In the pleasant air of noon,
Grows pale and blue with altered hue —
  In the gaze of the nightly moon;
For the planet of frost, so cold and bright,
Makes it wan with her borrowed light.

II.

Such is my heart — roses are fair,
  And that at best a withered blossom;
But thy false care did idly wear
  Its withered leaves in a faithless bosom;
And fed with love, like air and dew,
Its growth . . . .

SONNET.

OZYMANDIAS.

I MET a traveller from an antique land
Who said : Two vast and trunkless legs of stone
Stand in the desart. Near them, on the sand,
Half sunk, a shattered visage lies, whose frown,
And wrinkled lip, and sneer of cold command,
Tell that its sculptor well those passions read
Which yet survive, stamped on these lifeless things,
The hand that mocked them and the heart that fed :
And on the pedestal these words appear :
" My name is Ozymandias, king of kings :
Look on my works, ye Mighty, and despair ! "
Nothing beside remains. Round the decay
Of that colossal wreck, boundless and bare
The lone and level sands stretch far away.

"THAT TIME IS DEAD."

LINES.

I.

That time is dead for ever, child,
Drowned, frozen, dead for ever!
    We look on the past
    And stare aghast
At the spectres wailing, pale and ghast,
Of hopes which thou and I beguiled
    To death on life's dark river.

II.

The stream we gazed on then, rolled by;
Its waves are unreturning;
    But we yet stand
    In a lone land,
Like tombs to mark the memory
Of hopes and fears, which fade and flee
In the light of life's dim morning.

DEATH.

I.

They die — the dead return not — Misery
    Sits near an open grave and calls them over,
A Youth with hoary hair and haggard eye —
    They are the names of kindred, friend and lover,
Which he so feebly calls — they all are gone !
Fond wretch, all dead, those vacant names alone,
      This most familiar scene, my pain —
      These tombs alone remain.

II.

Misery, my sweetest friend — oh ! weep no more !
    Thou wilt not be consoled — I wonder not !
For I have seen thee from thy dwelling's door
    Watch the calm sunset with them, and this spot
Was even as bright and calm, but transitory,
And now thy hopes are gone, thy hair is hoary ;
      This most familiar scene, my pain —
      These tombs alone remain.

TO WILLIAM SHELLEY.

I.

The billows on the beach are leaping around it,
    The bark is weak and frail,
The sea looks black, and the clouds that bound it
    Darkly strew the gale.
Come with me, thou delightful child,
Come with me, though the wave is wild,
And the winds are loose, we must not stay,
Or the slaves of the law may rend thee away.

II.

They have taken thy brother and sister dear,
    They have made them unfit for thee;
They have withered the smile and dried the tear
    Which should have been sacred to me.
To a blighting faith and a cause of crime
They have bound them slaves in youthly prime,
And they will curse my name and thee
Because we are fearless and free.

III.

Come thou, belovèd as thou art;
    Another sleepeth still
Near thy sweet mother's anxious heart,
    Which thou with joy shalt fill,

With fairest smiles of wonder thrown
On that which is indeed our own,
And which in distant lands will be
The dearest playmate unto thee.

IV.

Fear not the tyrants will rule for ever,
   Or the priests of the evil faith;
They stand on the brink of that raging river,
   Whose waves they have tainted with death.
It is fed from the depth of a thousand dells,
Around them it foams and rages and swells;
And their swords and their sceptres I floating see,
Like wrecks on the surge of eternity.

V.

Rest, rest, and shriek not, thou gentle child!
   The rocking of the boat thou fearest,
And the cold spray and the clamour wild?—
   There sit between us two, thou dearest—
Me and thy mother—well we know
The storm at which thou tremblest so,
With all its dark and hungry graves,
Less cruel than the savage slaves
Who hunt us o'er these sheltering waves.

VI.

This hour will in thy memory
   Be a dream of days forgotten long,
We soon shall dwell by the azure sea
Of serene and golden Italy,
Or Greece, the Mother of the free;
   And I will teach thine infant tongue
To call upon those heroes old
In their own language, and will mould
Thy growing spirit in the flame
Of Grecian lore, that by such name
A patriot's birthright thou mayst claim!

LINES TO A CRITIC.

I.

Honey from silkworms who can gather,
   Or silk from the yellow bee?
The grass may grow in winter weather
   As soon as hate in me.

II.

Hate men who cant, and men who pray,
   And men who rail like thee;

TO MARY.

An equal passion to repay
   They are not coy like me.

III.

Or seek some slave of power and gold,
   To be thy dear heart's mate,
Thy love will move that bigot cold
   Sooner than me thy hate.

IV.

A passion like the one I prove
   Cannot divided be;
I hate thy want of truth and love —
   How should I then hate thee?

TO MARY ———.

O MARY dear, that you were here
With your brown eyes bright and clear,
And your sweet voice, like a bird
Singing love to its lone mate
In the ivy bower disconsolate;
Voice the sweetest ever heard!
And your brow more . . .

SONNET.

Than the   sky
Of this azure Italy.
Mary dear, come to me soon,
I am not well whilst thou art far;
As sunset to the spherèd moon,
As twilight to the western star,
Thou, belovèd, art to me.

O Mary dear, that you were here;
The Castle echo whispers "Here!"

SONNET.

LIFT not the painted veil which those who live
Call Life: though unreal shapes be pictured there,
And it but mimic all we would believe
With colours idly spread,— behind, lurk Fear
And Hope, twin destinies; who ever weave
Their shadows, o'er the chasm, sightless and drear.
I knew one who had lifted it — he sought,
For his lost heart was tender, things to love,
But found them not, alas! nor was there aught
The world contains, the which he could approve.

Through the unheeding many he did move,
A splendour among shadows, a bright blot
Upon this gloomy scene, a Spirit that strove
For truth, and like the Preacher found it not.

LINES WRITTEN AMONG THE EUGANEAN HILLS.

MANY a green isle needs must be
In the deep wide sea of misery,
Or the mariner, worn and wan,
Never thus could voyage on
Day and night, and night and day,
Drifting on his dreary way,
With the solid darkness black
Closing round his vessel's track;
Whilst above the sunless sky,
Big with clouds, hangs heavily,
And behind the tempest fleet
Hurries on with lightning feet,
Riving sail, and cord, and plank,
Till the ship has almost drank
Death from the o'er-brimming deep;
And sinks down, down, like that sleep
When the dreamer seems to be
Weltering through eternity;

LINES WRITTEN AMONG THE EUGANEAN HILLS.

And the dim low line before
Of a dark and distant shore
Still recedes, as ever still
Longing with divided will,
But no power to seek or shun,
He is ever drifted on
O'er the unreposing wave
To the haven of the grave.
What, if there no friends will greet;
What, if there no heart will meet
His with love's impatient beat;
Wander wheresoe'er he may,
Can he dream before that day
To find refuge from distress
In friendship's smile, in love's caress?
Then 'twill wreak him little woe
Whether such there be or no:
Senseless is the breast, and cold,
Which relenting love would fold;
Bloodless are the veins and chill
Which the pulse of pain did fill;
Every little living nerve
That from bitter words did swerve
Round the tortured lips and brow,
Are like sapless leaflets now
Frozen upon December's bough.

LINES WRITTEN AMONG THE EUGANEAN HILLS.

On the beach of a northern sea
Which tempests shake eternally,
As once the wretch there lay to sleep,
Lies a solitary heap,
One white skull and seven dry bones,
On the margin of the stones,
Where a few grey rushes stand,
Boundaries of the sea and land:
Nor is heard one voice of wail
But the sea-mews, as they sail
O'er the billows of the gale;
Or the whirlwind up and down
Howling, like a slaughtered town,
When a king in glory rides
Through the pomp of fratricides:
Those unburied bones around
There is many a mournful sound;
There is no lament for him,
Like a sunless vapour, dim,
Who once clothed with life and thought
What now moves nor murmurs not.

Aye, many flowering islands lie
In the waters of wide Agony:
To such a one this morn was led,
My bark by soft winds piloted:

LINES WRITTEN AMONG THE EUGANEAN HILLS.

'Mid the mountains Euganean
I stood listening to the pæan,
With which the legioned rooks did hail
The sun's uprise majestical;
Gathering round with wings all hoar,
Thro' the dewy mist they soar
Like grey shades, till the eastern heaven
Bursts, and then, as clouds of even,
Flecked with fire and azure, lie
In the unfathomable sky,
So their plumes of purple grain,
Starred with drops of golden rain,
Gleam above the sunlight woods,
As in silent multitudes
On the morning's fitful gale
Thro' the broken mist they sail,
And the vapours cloven and gleaming
Follow down the dark steep streaming,
Till all is bright, and clear, and still,
Round the solitary hill.

Beneath is spread like a green sea
The waveless plain of Lombardy,
Bounded by the vaporous air,
Islanded by cities fair;

LINES WRITTEN AMONG THE EUGANEAN HILLS.

Underneath day's azure eyes
Ocean's nursling, Venice lies,
A peopled labyrinth of walls,
Amphitrite's destined halls,
Which her hoary sire now paves
With his blue and beaming waves.
Lo! the sun upsprings behind,
Broad, red, radiant, half reclined
On the level quivering line
Of the waters crystalline;
And before that chasm of light,
As within a furnace bright,
Column, tower, and dome, and spire,
Shine like obelisks of fire,
Pointing with inconstant motion
From the altar of dark ocean
To the sapphire-tinted skies;
As the flames of sacrifice
From the marble shrines did rise,
As to pierce the dome of gold
Where Apollo spoke of old.

Sun-girt City, thou hast been
Ocean's child, and then his queen;
Now is come a darker day,
And thou soon must be his prey,

LINES WRITTEN AMONG THE EUGANEAN HILLS.

If the power that raised thee here
Hallow so thy watery bier.
A less drear ruin then than now,
With thy conquest-branded brow
Stooping to the slave of slaves
From thy throne, among the waves
Wilt thou be, when the sea-mew
Flies, as once before it flew,
O'er thine isles depopulate,
And all is in its antient state,
Save where many a palace gate
With green sea-flowers overgrown
Like a rock of ocean's own,
Topples o'er the abandoned sea
As the tides change sullenly.
The fisher on his watery way,
Wandering at the close of day,
Will spread his sail and seize his oar
Till he pass the gloomy shore,
Lest thy dead should, from their sleep
Bursting o'er the starlight deep,
Lead a rapid masque of death
O'er the waters of his path.

Those who alone thy towers behold
Quivering through aerial gold,

As I now behold them here,
Would imagine not they were
Sepulchres, where human forms,
Like pollution-nourished worms
To the corpse of greatness cling,
Murdered, and now mouldering:
But if Freedom should awake
In her omnipotence, and shake
From the Celtic Anarch's hold
All the keys of dungeons cold,
Where a hundred cities lie
Chained like thee, ingloriously,
Thou and all thy sister band
Might adorn this sunny land,
Twining memories of old time
With new virtues more sublime;
If not, perish thou and they,
Clouds which stain truth's rising day
By her sun consumed away,
Earth can spare ye: while like flowers,
In the waste of years and hours,
From your dust new nations spring
With more kindly blossoming.
Perish — let there only be
Floating o'er thy hearthless sea
As the garment of thy sky
Clothes the world immortally,

One remembrance, more sublime
Than the tattered pall of time,
Which scarce hides thy visage wan;—
That a tempest-cleaving Swan
Of the songs of Albion,
Driven from his ancestral streams
By the might of evil dreams,
Found a nest in thee; and Ocean
Welcomed him with such emotion
That its joy grew his, and sprung
From his lips like music flung
O'er a mighty thunder-fit
Chastening terror:—what though yet
Poesy's unfailing River,
Which thro' Albion winds for ever
Lashing with melodious wave
Many a sacred Poet's grave,
Mourn its latest nursling fled?
What though thou with all thy dead
Scarce can for this fame repay
Aught thine own? oh, rather say
Though thy sins and slaveries foul
Overcloud a sunlike soul?
As the ghost of Homer clings
Round Scamander's wasting springs;
As divinest Shakespeare's might
Fills Avon and the world with light

LINES WRITTEN AMONG THE EUGANEAN HILLS.

Like omniscient power which he
Imaged 'mid mortality;
As the love from Petrarch's urn,
Yet amid yon hills doth burn,
A quenchless lamp by which the heart
Sees things unearthly; — so thou art
Mighty spirit — so shall be
The City that did refuge thee.

Lo, the sun floats up the sky
Like thought-wingèd Liberty,
Till the universal light
Seems to level plain and height;
From the sea a mist has spread,
And the beams of morn lie dead
On the towers of Venice now,
Like its glory long ago.
By the skirts of that grey cloud
Many-domèd Padua proud
Stands, a peopled solitude,
'Mid the harvest shining plain,
Where the peasant heaps his grain
In the garner of his foe,
And the milk-white oxen slow
With the purple vintage strain,
Heaped upon the creaking wain,

That the brutal Celt may swill
Drunken sleep with savage will;
And the sickle to the sword
Lies unchanged, though many a lord,
Like a weed whose shade is poison,
Overgrows this region's foison,
Sheaves of whom are ripe to come
To destruction's harvest home:
Men must reap the things they sow,
Force from force must ever flow,
Or worse; but 'tis a bitter woe
That love or reason cannot change
The despot's rage, the slave's revenge.

Padua, thou within whose walls
Those mute guests at festivals,
Son and Mother, Death and Sin,
Played at dice for Ezzelin,
Till Death cried, "I win, I win!"
And Sin cursed to lose the wager,
But Death promised, to assuage her,
That he would petition for
Her to be made Vice-Emperor,
When the destined years were o'er,
Over all between the Po
And the eastern Alpine snow,

Under the mighty Austrian.
Sin smiled so as Sin only can,
And since that time, aye, long before,
Both have ruled from shore to shore,
That incestuous pair, who follow
Tyrants as the sun the swallow,
As Repentance follows Crime,
And as changes follow Time.

In thine halls the lamp of learning,
Padua, now no more is burning;
Like a meteor, whose wild way
Is lost over the grave of day,
It gleams betrayed and to betray:
Once remotest nations came
To adore that sacred flame,
When it lit not many a hearth
On this cold and gloomy earth:
Now new fires from antique light
Spring beneath the wide world's might;
But their spark lies dead in thee,
Trampled out by tyranny.
As the Norway woodman quells,
In the depth of piny dells,
One light flame among the brakes,
While the boundless forest shakes,

LINES WRITTEN AMONG THE EUGANEAN HILLS.

And its mighty trunks are torn
By the fire thus lowly born:
The spark beneath his feet is dead,
He starts to see the flames it fed
Howling through the darkened sky
With a myriad tongues victoriously,
And sinks down in fear: so thou,
O Tyranny, beholdest now
Light around thee, and thou hearest
The loud flames ascend, and fearest:
Grovel on the earth: aye, hide
In the dust thy purple pride!

Noon descends around me now:
'Tis the noon of autumn's glow,
When a soft and purple mist
Like a vaporous amethyst,
Or an air-dissolvèd star
Mingling light and fragrance, far
From the curved horizon's bound
To the point of heaven's profound,
Fills the overflowing sky;
And the plains that silent lie
Underneath, the leaves unsodden
Where the infant frost has trodden
With his morning-wingèd feet,
Whose bright print is gleaming yet;

LINES WRITTEN AMONG THE EUGANEAN HILLS.

And the red and golden vines,
Piercing with their trellised lines
The rough, dark-skirted wilderness;
The dun and bladed grass no less,
Pointing from this hoary tower
In the windless air; the flower
Glimmering at my feet; the line
Of the olive-sandalled Apennine
In the south dimly islanded;
And the Alps, whose snows are spread
High between the clouds and sun;
And of living things each one;
And my spirit which so long
Darkened this swift stream of song,
Interpenetrated lie
By the glory of the sky:
Be it love, light, harmony,
Odour, or the soul of all
Which from heaven like dew doth fall,
Or the mind which feeds this verse
Peopling the lone universe.
Noon descends, and after noon
Autumn's evening meets me soon,
Leading the infantine moon,
And that one star, which to her
Almost seems to minister

LINES WRITTEN AMONG THE EUGANEAN HILLS.

Half the crimson light she brings
From the sunset's radiant springs:
And the soft dreams of the morn,
(Which like wingèd winds had borne
To that silent isle, which lies
'Mid remembered agonies,
The frail bark of this lone being,)
Pass, to other sufferers fleeing,
And its ancient pilot, Pain,
Sits beside the helm again.

Other flowering isles must be
In the sea of life and agony:
Other spirits float and flee
O'er that gulph: even now, perhaps,
On some rock the wild wave wraps,
With folded wings they waiting sit
For my bark, to pilot it
To some calm and blooming cove,
Where for me, and those I love,
May a windless bower be built,
Far from passion, pain, and guilt,
In a dell 'mid lawny hills,
Which the wild sea-murmur fills,
And soft sunshine, and the sound
Of old forests echoing round,

And the light and smell divine
Of all flowers that breathe and shine:
We may live so happy there,
That the spirits of the air,
Envying us, may even entice
To our healing paradise
The polluting multitude;
But their rage would be subdued
By that clime divine and calm,
And the winds whose wings rain balm
On the uplifted soul, and leaves
Under which the bright sea heaves;
While each breathless interval
In their whisperings musical
The inspired soul supplies
With its own deep melodies,
And the love which heals all strife
Circling, like the breath of life,
All things in that sweet abode
With its own mild brotherhood:
They, not it would change; and soon
Every sprite beneath the moon
Would repent its envy vain,
And the earth grow young again.

JULIAN AND MADDALO:

A CONVERSATION.

I RODE one evening with Count Maddalo
Upon the bank of land which breaks the flow '
Of Adria towards Venice : a bare strand
Of hillocks, heaped from ever-shifting sand,
Matted with thistles and amphibious weeds,
Such as from earth's embrace the salt ooze breeds,
Is this ; an uninhabited sea-side,
Which the lone fisher, when his nets are dried,
Abandons ; and no other object breaks
The waste, but one dwarf tree and some few stakes
Broken and unrepaired, and the tide makes
A narrow space of level sand thereon,
Where 'twas our wont to ride while day went down.
This ride was my delight. I love all waste
And solitary places ; where we taste
The pleasure of believing what we see
Is boundless, as we wish our souls to be :
And such was this wide ocean, and this shore
More barren than its billows ; and yet more

Than all, with a remembered friend I love
To ride as then I rode;—for the winds drove
The living spray along the sunny air
Into our faces; the blue heavens were bare,
Stripped to their depths by the awakening north;
And, from the waves, sound like delight broke forth
Harmonizing with solitude, and sent
Into our hearts aërial merriment.
So, as we rode, we talked; and the swift thought,
Winging itself with laughter, lingered not,
But flew from brain to brain,—such glee was ours,
Charged with light memories of remembered hours,
None slow enough for sadness: till we came
Homeward, which always makes the spirit tame.
This day had been cheerful but cold, and now
The sun was sinking, and the wind also.
Our talk grew somewhat serious, as may be
Talk interrupted with such raillery
As mocks itself, because it cannot scorn
The thoughts it would extinguish:— 'twas forlorn,
Yet pleasing, such as once, so poets tell,
The devils held within the dales of Hell
Concerning God, freewill and destiny:
Of all that earth has been or yet may be,
All that vain men imagine or believe,
Or hope can paint or suffering may achieve,

We descanted, and I (for ever still
Is it not wise to make the best of ill?)
Argued against despondency, but pride
Made my companion take the darker side.
The sense that he was greater than his kind
Had struck, methinks, his eagle spirit blind
By gazing on its own exceeding light.
Meanwhile the sun paused ere it should alight,
Over the horizon of the mountains;—Oh
How beautiful is sunset, when the glow
Of Heaven descends upon a land like thee,
Thou Paradise of exiles, Italy!
Thy mountains, seas and vineyards and the towers
Of cities they encircle!—it was ours
To stand on thee, beholding it; and then
Just where we had dismounted the Count's men
Were waiting for us with the gondola.—
As those who pause on some delightful way
Tho' bent on pleasant pilgrimage, we stood
Looking upon the evening and the flood
Which lay between the city and the shore
Paved with the image of the sky . . . the hoar
And aëry Alps towards the North appeared
Thro' mist, an heaven-sustaining bulwark reared
Between the East and West; and half the sky
Was roofed with clouds of rich emblazonry

Dark purple at the zenith, which still grew
Down the steep West into a wondrous hue
Brighter than burning gold, even to the rent
Where the swift sun yet paused in his descent
Among the many folded hills : they were
Those famous Euganean hills, which bear
As seen from Lido thro' the harbour piles
The likeness of a clump of peakèd isles—
And then—as if the Earth and Sea had been
Dissolved into one lake of fire, were seen
Those mountains towering as from waves of flame
Around the vaporous sun, from which there came
The inmost purple spirit of light, and made
Their very peaks transparent. "Ere it fade,"
Said my companion, "I will show you soon
"A better station"—so, o'er the lagune
We glided, and from that funereal bark
I leaned, and saw the city, and could mark
How from their many isles in evening's gleam
Its temples and its palaces did seem
Like fabrics of enchantment piled to Heaven.
I was about to speak, when—"We are even
"Now at the point I meant," said Maddalo,
And bade the gondolieri cease to row.
"Look Julian on the west, and listen well
"If you hear not a deep and heavy bell."

I looked, and saw between us and the sun
A building on an island; such a one
As age to age might add, for uses vile,
A windowless, deformed and dreary pile;
And on the top an open tower, where hung
A bell, which in the radiance swayed and swung;
We could just hear its hoarse and iron tongue:
The broad sun sunk behind it, and it tolled
In strong and black relief.—"What we behold
"Shall be the madhouse and its belfry tower,"
Said Maddalo, "and ever at this hour
"Those who may cross the water, hear that bell
"Which calls the maniacs each one from his cell
"To vespers."—"As much skill as need to pray
"In thanks or hope for their dark lot have they
"To their stern maker," I replied. "O ho!
"You talk as in years past," said Maddalo.
"'Tis strange men change not. You were ever still
"Among Christ's flock a perilous infidel,
"A wolf for the meek lambs—if you can't swim
"Beware of Providence." I looked on him,
But the gay smile had faded in his eye,
"And such,"—he cried, "is our mortality,
"And this must be the emblem and the sign
"Of what should be eternal and divine!—
"And like that black and dreary bell, the soul
"Hung in a heaven-illumined tower, must toll

" Our thoughts and our desires to meet below
" Round the rent heart and pray — as madmen do
" For what? they know not, till the night of death
" As sunset that strange vision, severeth
" Our memory from itself, and us from all
" We sought and yet were baffled." I recall
The sense of what he said, altho' I mar
The force of his expressions. The broad star
Of day meanwhile had sunk behind the hill,
And the black bell became invisible,
And the red tower looked grey, and all between
The churches, ships and palaces were seen
Huddled in gloom; — into the purple sea
The orange hues of heaven sunk silently.
We hardly spoke, and soon the gondola
Conveyed me to my lodgings by the way.

   The following morn was rainy, cold and dim,
Ere Maddalo arose, I called on him,
And whilst I waited with his child I played;
A lovelier toy sweet Nature never made,
A serious, subtle, wild, yet gentle being,
Graceful without design and unforeseeing,
With eyes — Oh speak not of her eyes ! — which seem
Twin mirrors of Italian Heaven, yet gleam
With such deep meaning, as we never see
But in the human countenance: with me

She was a special favourite, I had nursed
Her fine and feeble limbs when she came first
To this bleak world; and she yet seemed to know
On second sight her antient playfellow,
Less changed than she was by six months or so;
For after her first shyness was worn out
We sate there, rolling billiard balls about,
When the Count entered — salutations past;
" The words you spoke last night might well have
" A darkness on my spirit — if man be
" The passive thing you say, I should not see
" Much harm in the religions and old saws
" (Tho' I may never own such leaden laws)
" Which break a teachless nature to the yoke:
" Mine is another faith " — thus much I spoke
And noting he replied not, added: " See
" This lovely child, blithe, innocent and free,
" She spends a happy time with little care
" While we to such sick thoughts subjected are
" As came on you last night — it is our will
" That thus enchains us to permitted ill —
" We might be otherwise — we might be all
" We dream of happy, high, majestical.
" Where is the love, beauty and truth we seek.
" But in our mind? and if we were not weak
" Should we be less in deed than in desire?"
" Aye, if we were not weak — and we aspire

"How vainly to be strong!" said Maddalo:
"You talk Utopia." "It remains to know,"
I then rejoined, "and those who try may find
"How strong the chains are which our spirit bind;
"Brittle perchance as straw ... We are assured
"Much may be conquered, much may be endured
"Of what degrades and crushes us. We know
"That we have power over ourselves to do
"And suffer — what, we know not till we try;
"But something nobler than to live and die —
"So taught those kings of old philosophy
"Who reigned, before Religion made men blind;
"And those who suffer with their suffering kind
"Yet feel their faith, religion." "My dear friend,"
Said Maddalo, "my judgment will not bend
"To your opinion, tho' I think you might
"Make such a system refutation-tight
"As far as words go. I knew one like you
"Who to this city came some months ago,
"With whom I argued in this sort, and he
"Is now gone mad, — and so he answered me, —
"Poor fellow! but if you would like to go
"We'll visit him, and his wild talk will shew
"How vain are such aspiring theories."
"I hope to prove the induction otherwise,
"And that a want of that true theory, still,
"Which seeks a 'soul of goodness' in things ill,

"Or in himself or others, has thus bowed
"His being — there are some by nature proud,
"Who patient in all else demand but this:
"To love and be beloved with gentleness;
"And being scorned, what wonder if they die
"Some living death? this is not destiny
"But man's own wilful ill."

                        As thus I spoke
Servants announced the gondola, and we
Through the fast-falling rain and high-wrought sea
Sailed to the island where the madhouse stands.
We disembarked. The clap of tortured hands,
Fierce yells and howlings and lamentings keen,
And laughter where complaint had merrier been,
Moans, shrieks, and curses, and blaspheming prayers
Accosted us. We climbed the oozy stairs
Into an old court yard. I heard on high,
Then, fragments of most touching melody,
But looking up saw not the singer there —
Through the black bars in the tempestuous air
I saw, like weeds on a wrecked palace growing,
Long tangled locks flung wildly forth, and flowing,
Of those who on a sudden were beguiled
Into strange silence, and looked forth and smiled
Hearing sweet sounds. — Then I: "Methinks there we
"A cure of these with patience and kind care,

If music can thus move ... but what is he
Whom we seek here?" "Of his sad history
I know but this," said Maddalo, "he came
To Venice a dejected man, and fame
Said he was wealthy, or he had been so;
Some thought the loss of fortune wrought him woe;
But he was ever talking in such sort
As you do — far more sadly — he seemed hurt,
Even as a man with his peculiar wrong,
To hear but of the oppression of the strong,
Or those absurd deceits (I think with you
In some respects you know) which carry through
The excellent impostors of this earth
When they outface detection — he had worth,
Poor fellow! but a humorist in his way" —
Alas, what drove him mad?" "I cannot say;
A lady came with him from France, and when
She left him and returned, he wandered then
About yon lonely isles of desart sand
Till he grew wild — he had no cash or land
Remaining, — the police had brought him here —
Some fancy took him and he would not bear
Removal; so I fitted up for him
Those rooms beside the sea, to please his whim,
And sent him busts and books and urns for flowers
Which had adorned his life in happier hours,

"And instruments of music — you may guess
"A stranger could do little more or less
"For one so gentle and unfortunate,
"And those are his sweet strains which charm the weight
"From madmen's chains, and make this Hell appear
"A heaven of sacred silence, hushed to hear." —
"Nay, this was kind of you — he had no claim,
As the world says" — "None — but the very same
"Which I on all mankind were I as he
"Fallen to such deep reverse ; — his melody
"Is interrupted — now we hear the din
"Of madmen, shriek on shriek again begin ;
"Let us now visit him ; after this strain
"He ever communes with himself again,
"And sees nor hears not any." Having said
These words we called the keeper, and he led
To an apartment opening on the sea —
There the poor wretch was sitting mournfully
Near a piano, his pale fingers twined
One with the other, and the ooze and wind
Rushed thro' an open casement, and did sway
His hair, and starred it with the brackish spray ;
His head was leaning on a music book,
And he was muttering, and his lean limbs shook ;
His lips were pressed against a folded leaf
In hue too beautiful for health, and grief

JULIAN AND MADDALO.

Smiled in their motions as they lay apart —
As one who wrought from his own fervid heart
The eloquence of passion, soon he raised
His sad meek face and eyes lustrous and glazed
And spoke — sometimes as one who wrote and thought
His words might move some heart that heeded not
If sent to distant lands : and then as one
Reproaching deeds never to be undone
With wondering self-compassion ; then his speech
Was lost in grief, and then his words came each
Unmodulated, cold, expressionless ;
But that from one jarred accent you might guess
It was despair made them so uniform :
And all the while the loud and gusty storm
Hissed thro' the window, and we stood behind
Stealing his accents from the envious wind
Unseen. I yet remember what he said
Distinctly : such impression his words made.

'Month after month,' he cried, 'to bear this load
And as a jade urged by the whip and goad
To drag life on, which like a heavy chain
Lengthens behind with many a link of pain ! —
And not to speak my grief — O not to dare
To give a human voice to my despair,
But live and move, and wretched thing ! smile on
As if I never went aside to groan,

And wear this mask of falsehood even to those
Who are most dear — not for my own repose —
Alas no scorn or pain or hate could be
So heavy as that falsehood is to me —
But that I cannot bear more altered faces
Than needs must be, more changed and cold embraces,
More misery, disappointment and mistrust
To own me for their father ... Would the dust
Were covered in upon my body now!
That the life ceased to toil within my brow!
And then these thoughts would at the least be fled;
Let us not fear such pain can vex the dead.

'What Power delights to torture us? I know
That to myself I do not wholly owe
What now I suffer, tho' in part I may.
Alas none strewed sweet flowers upon the way
Where wandering heedlessly, I met pale Pain
My shadow, which will leave me not again —
If I have erred, there was no joy in error,
But pain and insult and unrest and terror;
I have not as some do, bought penitence
With pleasure, and a dark yet sweet offence,
For then, — if love and tenderness and truth
Had overlived hope's momentary youth,
My creed should have redeemed me from repenting,
But loathèd scorn and outrage unrelenting

Met love excited by far other seeming
Until the end was gained ... as one from dreaming
Of sweetest peace, I woke, and found my state
Such as it is. ——

    'O Thou, my spirit's mate
Who, for thou art compassionate and wise,
Wouldst pity me from thy most gentle eyes
If this sad writing thou shouldst ever see —
My secret groans must be unheard by thee,
Thou wouldst weep tears bitter as blood to know
Thy lost friend's incommunicable woe.

 'Ye few by whom my nature has been weighed
In friendship, let me not that name degrade
By placing on your hearts the secret load
Which crushes mine to dust. There is one road
To peace and that is truth, which follow ye!
Love sometimes leads astray to misery.
Yet think not tho' subdued — and I may well
Say that I am subdued — that the full Hell
Within me would infect the untainted breast
Of sacred nature with its own unrest;
As some perverted beings think to find
In scorn or hate a medicine for the mind
Which scorn or hate have wounded — O how vain!
The dagger heals not but may rend again ....

Believe that I am ever still the same
In creed as in resolve, and what may tame
My heart, must leave the understanding free,
Or all would sink in this keen agony —
Nor dream that I will join the vulgar cry,
Or with my silence sanction tyranny,
Or seek a moment's shelter from my pain
In any madness which the world calls gain,
Ambition or revenge or thoughts as stern
As those which make me what I am, or turn
To avarice or misanthropy or lust ....
Heap on me soon, O grave, thy welcome dust!
Till then the dungeon may demand its prey,
And Poverty and Shame may meet and say —
Halting beside me on the public way —
That love-devoted youth is our's — let's sit
Beside him — he may live some six months yet.
Or the red scaffold, as our country bends,
May ask some willing victim, or ye friends
May fall under some sorrow which this heart
Or hand may share or vanquish or avert;
I am prepared: in truth with no proud joy
To do or suffer aught, as when a boy
I did devote to justice and to love
My nature, worthless now! ...

'I must remove
A veil from my pent mind. 'Tis torn aside!
O, pallid as Death's dedicated bride,
Thou mockery which art sitting by my side,
Am I not wan like thee? at the grave's call
I haste, invited to thy wedding-ball
To greet the ghastly paramour, for whom
Thou hast deserted me . . . and made the tomb
Thy bridal bed . . . but I beside your feet
Will lie and watch ye from my winding sheet —
Thus . . . wide awake tho' dead . . . yet stay O stay!
Go not so soon — I know not what I say —
Hear but my reasons . . I am mad, I fear,
My fancy is o'erwrought . . thou art not here . . .
Pale art thou, 'tis most true . . but thou art gone,
Thy work is finished . . . I am left alone!—

* * * * *

'Nay, was it I who wooed thee to this breast
Which, like a serpent thou envenomest
As in repayment of the warmth it lent?
Didst thou not seek me for thine own content?
Did not thy love awaken mine? I thought
That thou wert she who said "You kiss me not
Ever, I fear you do not love me now"—
In truth I loved even to my overthrow

Her, who would fain forget these words: but they
Cling to her mind, and cannot pass away.

* * * * *

'You say that I am proud — that when I speak
My lip is tortured with the wrongs which break
The spirit it expresses ... Never one
Humbled himself before, as I have done!
Even the instinctive worm on which we tread
Turns, tho' it wound not — then with prostrate head
Sinks in the dust and writhes like me — and dies?
No: wears a living death of agonies!
As the slow shadows of the pointed grass
Mark the eternal periods, his pangs pass
Slow, ever-moving, — making moments be
As mine seem — each an immortality!

* * * * *

'That you had never seen me — never heard
My voice, and more than all had ne'er endured
The deep pollution of my loathed embrace —
That your eyes ne'er had lied love in my face —
That, like some maniac monk, I had torn out
The nerves of manhood by their bleeding root
With mine own quivering fingers, so that ne'er
Our hearts had for a moment mingled there
To disunite in horror — these were not
With thee, like some suppressed and hideous thought

Which flits athwart our musings, but can find
No rest within a pure and gentle mind . . .
Thou sealedst them with many a bare broad word
And searedst my memory o'er them, — for I heard
And can forget not . . . . they were ministered
One after one, those curses. Mix them up
Like self-destroying poisons in one cup,
And they will make one blessing which thou ne'er
Didst imprecate for, on me, — death.

   * * * * *

      'It were
A cruel punishment for one most cruel
If such can love, to make that love the fuel
Of the mind's hell; hate, scorn, remorse, despair:
But *me* — whose heart a stranger's tear might wear
As water-drops the sandy fountain-stone,
Who loved and pitied all things, and could moan
For woes which others hear not, and could see
The absent with the glance of phantasy,
And with the poor and trampled sit and weep,
Following the captive to his dungeon deep;
Me — who am as a nerve o'er which do creep
The else unfelt oppressions of this earth,
And was to thee the flame upon thy hearth,
When all beside was cold — that thou on me
Shouldst rain these plagues of blistering agony —

Such curses are from lips once eloquent
With love's too partial praise — let none relent
Who intend deeds too dreadful for a name
Henceforth, if an example for the same
They seek ... for thou on me lookedst so, and so —
And didst speak thus .. and thus ... I live to shew
How much men bear and die not!

   * * * * *

         'Thou wilt tell
With the grimace of hate how horrible
It was to meet my love when thine grew less;
Thou wilt admire how I could e'er address
Such features to love's work ... this taunt, tho' true,
(For indeed nature nor in form nor hue
Bestowed on me her choicest workmanship)
Shall not be thy defence ... for since thy lip
Met mine first, years long past, since thine eye kindled
With soft fire under mine, I have not dwindled
Nor changed in mind or body, or in aught
But as love changes what it loveth not
After long years and many trials.

          'How vain
Are words! I thought never to speak again,
Not even in secret, — not to my own heart —
But from my lips the unwilling accents start,

And from my pen the words flow as I write,
Dazzling my eyes with scalding tears . . . my sight
Is dim to see that charactered in vain
On this unfeeling leaf which burns the brain
And eats into it . . . blotting all things fair
And wise and good which time had written there.

'Those who inflict must suffer, for they see
The work of their own hearts and this must be
Our chastisement or recompense — O child!
I would that thine were like to be more mild
For both our wretched sakes . . . for thine the most
Who feelest already all that thou hast lost
Without the power to wish it thine again;
And as slow years pass, a funereal train
Each with the ghost of some lost hope or friend
Following it like its shadow, wilt thou bend
No thought on my dead memory?

*   *   *   *   *

      'Alas, love!
Fear me not . . . against thee I would not move
A finger in despite. Do I not live
That thou mayst have less bitter cause to grieve?
I give thee tears for scorn and love for hate;
And that thy lot may be less desolate
Than his on whom thou tramplest, I refrain
From that sweet sleep which medicines all pain.

Then, when thou speakest of me, never say
He could forgive not. Here I cast away
All human passions, all revenge, all pride;
I think, speak, act no ill; I do but hide
Under these words like embers, every spark
Of that which has consumed me — quick and dark
The grave is yawning . . . as its roof shall cover
My limbs with dust and worms under and over.
So let Oblivion hide this grief . . . the air
Closes upon my accents, as despair
Upon my heart — let death upon despair!'

   He ceased, and overcome leant back awhile,
Then rising, with a melancholy smile
Went to a sofa, and lay down, and slept
A heavy sleep, and in his dreams he wept
And muttered some familiar name, and we
Wept without shame in his society.
I think I never was impressed so much;
The man who were not, must have lacked a touch
Of human nature . . . then we lingered not,
Although our argument was quite forgot,
But calling the attendants, went to dine
At Maddalo's; yet neither cheer nor wine
Could give us spirits, for we talked of him
And nothing else, till daylight made stars dim;

And we agreed his was some dreadful ill
Wrought on him bodily, yet unspeakable,
By a dear friend; some deadly change in love
Of one vowed deeply which he dreamed not of;
For whose sake he, it seemed, had fixed a blot
Of falsehood on his mind which flourished not
But in the light of all-beholding truth,
And having stamped this canker on his youth
She had abandoned him — and how much more
Might be his woe, we guessed not — he had store
Of friends and fortune once, as we could guess
From his nice habits and his gentleness;
These were now lost . . . it were a grief indeed
If he had changed one unsustaining reed
For all that such a man might else adorn.
The colours of his mind seemed yet unworn;
For the wild language of his grief was high,
Such as in measure were called poetry,
And I remember one remark which then
Maddalo made. He said: "Most wretched men
Are cradled into poetry by wrong,
They learn in suffering what they teach in song."

If I had been an unconnected man
I, from this moment, should have formed some plan
Never to leave sweet Venice, — for to me
It was delight to ride by the lone sea;

And then, the town is silent — one may write
Or read in gondolas by day or night,
Having the little brazen lamp alight,
Unseen, uninterrupted ; books are there,
Pictures, and casts from all those statues fair
Which were twin-born with poetry, and all
We seek in towns, with little to recall
Regrets for the green country. I might sit
In Maddalo's great palace, and his wit
And subtle talk would cheer the winter night
And make me know myself, and the firelight
Would flash upon our faces, till the day
Might dawn and make me wonder at my stay :
But I had friends in London too : the chief
Attraction here, was that I sought relief
From the deep tenderness that maniac wrought
Within me — 'twas perhaps an idle thought —
But I imagined that if day by day
I watched him, and but seldom went away,
And studied all the beatings of his heart
With zeal, as men study some stubborn art
For their own good, and could by patience find
An entrance to the caverns of his mind,
I might reclaim him from this dark estate :
In friendships I had been most fortunate —
Yet never saw I one whom I would call
More willingly my friend ; and this was all

Accomplished not; such dreams of baseless good
Oft come and go in crowds and solitude
And leave no trace — but what I now designed
Made for long years impression on my mind.
The following morning urged by my affairs
I left bright Venice.

     After many years
And many changes I returned; the name
Of Venice, and it's aspect was the same;
But Maddalo was travelling far away
Among the mountains of Armenia.
His dog was dead. His child had now become
A woman; such as it has been my doom
To meet with few, a wonder of this earth
Where there is little of transcendant worth,
Like one of Shakespeare's women: kindly she,
And with a manner beyond courtesy,
Received her father's friend; and when I asked
Of the lorn maniac, she her memory tasked
And told as she had heard the mournful tale.
" That the poor sufferer's health began to fail
" Two years from my departure, but that then
" The lady who had left him, came again.
" Her mien had been imperious, but she now
" Looked meek — perhaps remorse had brought her low.

"Her coming made him better, and they stayed
"Together at my father's — for I played
"As I remember with the lady's shawl —
"I might be six years old — but after all
"She left him" . . . "Why, her heart must have been
    tough:
"How did it end?" "And was not this enough?
"They met — they parted" — "Child, is there no
    more?"
"Something within that interval which bore
"The stamp of *why* they parted, *how* they met:
"Yet if thine agèd eyes disdain to wet
"Those wrinkled cheeks with youth's remembered tears,
"Ask me no more, but let the silent years
"Be closed and cered over their memory
"As yon mute marble where their corpses lie."
I urged and questioned still, she told me how
All happened — but the cold world shall not know.

SONG,

ON A FADED VIOLET.

I.

The odour from the flower is gone,
  Which like thy kisses breathed on me;
The colour from the flower is flown,
  Which glowed of thee, and only thee!

II.

A shrivelled, lifeless, vacant form,
  It lies on my abandoned breast,
And mocks the heart which yet is warm
  With cold and silent rest.

III.

I weep — my tears revive it not!
  I sigh — it breathes no more on me;
Its mute and uncomplaining lot
  Is such as mine should be.

STANZAS.

WRITTEN IN DEJECTION, NEAR NAPLES.

I.

The sun is warm, the sky is clear,
    The waves are dancing fast and bright,
Blue isles and snowy mountains wear
    The purple noon's transparent might,
    The breath of the moist earth is light,
Around its unexpanded buds;
    Like many a voice of one delight,
The winds, the birds, the ocean floods,
The City's voice itself is soft like Solitude's.

II.

I see the Deep's untrampled floor
    With green and purple seaweed strown;
I see the waves upon the shore,
    Like light dissolved in star-showers, thrown:
    I sit upon the sands alone,
The lightning of the noon-tide ocean
    Is flashing round me, and a tone
Arises from its measured motion,
How sweet! did any heart now share in my emotion.

STANZAS IN DEJECTION.

III.

Alas! I have nor hope nor health,
    Nor peace within nor calm around,
Nor that content surpassing wealth
    The sage in meditation found,
    And walked with inward glory crowned —
Nor fame, nor power, nor love, nor leisure.
    Others I see whom these surround —
Smiling they live and call life pleasure; —
To me that cup has been dealt in another measure.

IV.

Yet now despair itself is mild,
    Even as the winds and waters are;
I could lie down like a tired child,
    And weep away the life of care
    Which I have borne and yet must bear,
Till death like sleep might steal on me,
    And I might feel in the warm air
My cheek grow cold, and hear the sea
Breathe o'er my dying brain its last monotony.

V.

Some might lament that I were cold,
    As I, when this sweet day is gone,
Which my lost heart, too soon grown old,
    Insults with this untimely moan;

They might lament — for I am one
Whom men love not, — and yet regret,
Unlike this day, which, when the sun
Shall on its stainless glory set,
Will linger, though enjoyed, like joy in memory yet.

THE PAST.

I.

WILT thou forget the happy hours
Which we buried in Love's sweet bowers,
Heaping over their corpses cold
Blossoms and leaves, instead of mould?
    Blossoms which were the joys that fell,
        And leaves, the hopes that yet remain.

II.

Forget the dead, the past? O yet
There are ghosts that may take revenge for it,
Memories that make the heart a tomb,
Regrets which glide through the spirit's gloom,
    And with ghastly whispers tell
        That joy, once lost, is pain.

PASSAGE OF THE APENNINES.

LISTEN, listen, Mary mine,
To the whisper of the Apennine,
It bursts on the roof like the thunder's roar,
Or like the sea on a northern shore,
Heard in its raging ebb and flow
By the captives pent in the cave below.
The Apennine in the light of day
Is a mighty mountain dim and grey,
Which between the earth and sky doth lay;
But when night comes, a chaos dread
On the dim starlight then is spread,
And the Apennine walks abroad with the storm.

INVOCATION TO MISERY.

I.

COME, be happy!— sit by me,
Shadow-vested Misery:
Coy, unwilling, silent bride,
Mourning in thy robe of pride,
Desolation — deified!

II.

Come, be happy! — sit near me:
Sad as I may seem to thee,
I am happier far than thou,
Lady, whose imperial brow
Is endiademed with woe.

III.

Misery! we have known each other,
Like a sister and a brother
Living in the same lone home,
Many years — we must live some
Hours or ages yet to come.

IV.

'Tis an evil lot, and yet
Let us make the best of it;
If love lives when pleasure dies,
We will love, till in our eyes
This heart's Hell seem Paradise.

V.

Come, be happy! — lie thee down
On the fresh grass newly mown,
Where the Grasshopper doth sing
Merrily — one joyous thing
In a world of sorrowing!

VI.

There our tent shall be the willow,
And thine arm shall be my pillow;
Sounds and odours sorrowful
Because they once were sweet, shall lull
Us to slumber, deep and dull.

VII.

Ha! thy frozen pulses flutter
With a love thou darest not utter.
Thou art murmuring — thou art weeping —
Is thine icy bosom leaping
While my burning heart lies sleeping?

VIII.

Kiss me; — oh! thy lips are cold:
Round my neck thine arms enfold —
They are soft, but chill and dead;
And thy tears upon my head
Burn like points of frozen lead.

IX.

Hasten to the bridal bed —
Underneath the grave 'tis spread:
In darkness may our love be hid,
Oblivion be our coverlid —
We may rest, and none forbid.

X.

Clasp me till our hearts be grown
Like two shadows into one;
Till this dreadful transport may
Like a vapour fade away,
In the sleep that lasts alway.

XI.

We may dream, in that long sleep,
That we are not those who weep;
E'en as Pleasure dreams of thee,
Life-deserting Misery,
Thou mayst dream of her with me.

XII.

Let us laugh, and make our mirth,
At the shadows of the earth,
As dogs bay the moonlight clouds,
Which, like spectres wrapt in shrouds,
Pass o'er night in multitudes.

XIII.

All the wide world, beside us
Show like multitudinous
Puppets passing from a scene;
What but mockery can they mean,
Where I am — where thou hast been?

SONG FOR "TASSO."

I.

I LOVED — alas! our life is love;
But when we cease to breathe and move
I do suppose love ceases too.
I thought, but not as now I do,
Keen thoughts and bright of linkèd lore,
Of all that men had thought before,
And all that nature shows, and more.

II.

And still I love and still I think,
But strangely, for my heart can drink
The dregs of such despair, and live,
And love;
And if I think, my thoughts come fast,
I mix the present with the past,
And each seems uglier than the last.

III.

Sometimes I see before me flee
A silver spirit's form, like thee,
O Leonora, and I sit
Still watching it,

Till by the grated casement's ledge
It fades, with such a sigh, as sedge
Breathes o'er the breezy streamlet's edge.

ODE TO HEAVEN.

CHORUS OF SPIRITS.

FIRST SPIRIT.

PALACE-ROOF of cloudless nights!
Paradise of golden lights!
   Deep, immeasurable, vast,
Which art now, and which wert then!
   Of the present and the past,
Of the eternal where and when,
   Presence-chamber, temple, home,
   Ever-canopying dome,
   Of acts and ages yet to come!

Glorious shapes have life in thee,
Earth, and all earth's company;
   Living globes which ever throng
Thy deep chasms and wildernesses;
   And green worlds that glide along;
And swift stars with flashing tresses;
   And icy moons most cold and bright,
   And mighty suns beyond the night,
   Atoms of intensest light.

ODE TO HEAVEN.

Even thy name is as a god,
Heaven! for thou art the abode
  Of that power which is the glass
Wherein man his nature sees.
  Generations as they pass
Worship thee with bended knees.
  Their unremaining gods and they
  Like a river roll away:
  Thou remainest such alway.

SECOND SPIRIT.

Thou art but the mind's first chamber,
Round which its young fancies clamber,
  Like weak insects in a cave,
Lighted up by stalactites;
  But the portal of the grave,
Where a world of new delights
  Will make thy best glories seem
  But a dim and noonday gleam
  From the shadow of a dream!

THIRD SPIRIT.

Peace! the abyss is wreathed with scorn
At your presumption, atom-born!
  What is heaven? and what are ye
Who its brief expanse inherit?

AN EXHORTATION.

What are suns and spheres which flee
With the instinct of that spirit
  Of which ye are but a part?
  Drops which Nature's mighty heart
  Drives through thinnest veins. Depart!

What is heaven? a globe of dew,
Filling in the morning new
  Some eyed flower whose young leaves waken
On an unimagined world:
  Constellated suns unshaken,
Orbits measureless, are furled
  In that frail and fading sphere,
  With ten millions gathered there,
  To tremble, gleam, and disappear.

AN EXHORTATION.

CAMELIONS feed on light and air:
  Poets' food is love and fame:
If in this wide world of care
  Poets could but find the same
With as little toil as they,
  Would they ever change their hue

AN EXHORTATION.

    As the light camelions do,
Suiting it to every ray
Twenty times a-day?

Poets are on this cold earth,
    As camelions might be,
Hidden from their early birth
    In a cave beneath the sea;
Where light is camelions change:
    Where love is not, poets do:
    Fame is love disguised: if few
Find either never think it strange
That poets range.

Yet dare not stain with wealth or power
    A poet's free and heavenly mind:
If bright camelions should devour
    Any food but beams and wind,
They would grow as earthly soon
    As their brother lizards are.
    Children of a sunnier star,
Spirits from beyond the moon,
O, refuse the boon!

ODE TO THE WEST WIND.

I.

O, WILD West Wind, thou breath of Autumn's being,
Thou, from whose unseen presence the leaves dead
Are driven, like ghosts from an enchanter fleeing,

Yellow, and black, and pale, and hectic red,
Pestilence-stricken multitudes : O, thou,
Who chariotest to their dark wintry bed

The wingèd seeds, where they lie cold and low,
Each like a corpse within its grave, until
Thine azure sister of the spring shall blow

Her clarion o'er the dreaming earth, and fill
(Driving sweet buds like flocks to feed in air)
With living hues and odours plain and hill :

Wild Spirit, which art moving every where ;
Destroyer and preserver ; hear, O, hear !

II.

Thou on whose stream, 'mid the steep sky's commotio
Loose clouds like earth's decaying leaves are shed,
Shook from the tangled boughs of Heaven and Ocea

ODE TO WEST WIND.

Angels of rain and lightning: there are spread
On the blue surface of thine airy surge,
Like the bright hair uplifted from the head

Of some fierce Mænad, even from the dim verge
Of the horizon to the zenith's height
The locks of the approaching storm. Thou dirge

Of the dying year, to which this closing night
Will be the dome of a vast sepulchre,
Vaulted with all thy congregated might

Of vapours, from whose solid atmosphere
Black rain, and fire, and hail will burst: O, hear!

III.

Thou who didst waken from his summer dreams
The blue Mediterranean, where he lay,
Lulled by the coil of his crystàlline streams,

Beside a pumice isle in Baiæ's bay,
And saw in sleep old palaces and towers
Quivering within the wave's intenser day,

All overgrown with azure moss and flowers
So sweet, the sense faints picturing them! Thou
For whose path the Atlantic's level powers

Cleave themselves into chasms, while far below
The sea-blooms and the oozy woods which wear
The sapless foliage of the ocean, know

Thy voice, and suddenly grow grey with fear,
And tremble and despoil themselves : O, hear !

IV.

If I were a dead leaf thou mightest bear ;
If I were a swift cloud to fly with thee ;
A wave to pant beneath thy power, and share

The impulse of thy strength, only less free
Than thou, O, uncontroulable ! If even
I were as in my boyhood, and could be

The comrade of thy wanderings over heaven,
As then, when to outstrip thy skiey speed
Scarce seemed a vision ; I would ne'er have striven

As thus with thee in prayer in my sore need.
Oh ! lift me as a wave, a leaf, a cloud !
I fall upon the thorns of life ! I bleed !

A heavy weight of hours has chained and bowed
One too like thee : tameless, and swift, and proud.

ODE TO WEST WIND.

V.

Make me thy lyre, even as the forest is :
What if my leaves are falling like its own !
The tumult of thy mighty harmonies

Will take from both a deep, autumnal tone,
Sweet though in sadness. Be thou, spirit fierce,
My spirit ! Be thou me, impetuous one !

Drive my dead thoughts over the universe
Like withered leaves to quicken a new birth !
And, by the incantation of this verse,

Scatter, as from an unextinguished hearth
Ashes and sparks, my words among mankind !
Be through my lips to unawakened earth

The trumpet of a prophecy ! O, wind,
If Winter comes, can Spring be far behind ?

AN ODE,

[WRITTEN, OCTOBER, 1819, BEFORE THE SPANIARDS HAD RECOVERED THEIR LIBERTY.]

  ARISE, arise, arise!
 There is blood on the earth that denies ye bread
  Be your wounds like eyes
 To weep for the dead, the dead, the dead.
What other grief were it just to pay?
Your sons, your wives, your brethren, were they;
Who said they were slain on the battle day?

  Awaken, awaken, awaken!
 The slave and the tyrant are twin-born foes;
  Be the cold chains shaken
 To the dust where your kindred repose, repose:
Their bones in the grave will start and move,
When they hear the voices of those they love,
Most loud in the holy combat above.

  Wave, wave high the banner!
 When Freedom is riding to conquest by:
  Though the slaves that fan her
 Be Famine and Toil, giving sigh for sigh.

ODE TO ASSERTORS OF LIBERTY.

And ye who attend her imperial car,
Lift not your hands in the banded war,
But in her defence whose children ye are.

    Glory, glory, glory,
  To those who have greatly suffered and done !
    Never name in story
  Was greater than that which ye shall have won.
Conquerors have conquered their foes alone,
Whose revenge, pride, and power they have overthrown :
Ride ye, more victorious, over your own.

    Bind, bind every brow
  With crownals of violet, ivy, and pine :
    Hide the blood-stains now
  With hues which sweet nature has made divine :
Green strength, azure hope, and eternity :
But let not the pansy among them be ;
Ye were injured, and that means memory.

THE INDIAN SERENADE.

I.

I ARISE from dreams of thee
In the first sweet sleep of night,
When the winds are breathing low,
And the stars are shining bright:
I arise from dreams of thee,
And a spirit in my feet
Hath led me — who knows how?
To thy chamber window, Sweet!

II.

The wandering airs they faint
On the dark, the silent stream —
And the Champak's odours fail
Like sweet thoughts in a dream;
The nightingale's complaint,
It dies upon her heart; —
As I must on thine,
O! belovèd as thou art!

III.

O lift me from the grass!
I die! I faint! I fail!

TO SOPHIA STACEY.

Let thy love in kisses rain
On my lips and eyelids pale.
My cheek is cold and white, alas!
My heart beats loud and fast;—
Oh! press it to thine own again,
Where it will break at last.

TO SOPHIA.

I.

Thou art fair, and few are fairer,
  Of the nymphs of earth or ocean.
They are robes that fit the wearer—
  Those soft limbs of thine, whose motion
Ever falls and shifts and glances,
As the life within them dances.

II.

Thy deep eyes, a double planet,
  Gaze the wisest into madness
With soft clear fire. The winds that fan it
  Are those thoughts of gentle gladness
Which, like zephyrs on the billow,
Make thy gentle soul their pillow.

TO SOPHIA STACEY.

III.

If whatever face thou paintest
   In those eyes grows pale with pleasure,
If the fainting soul is faintest
   When it hears thy harp's wild measure,
Wonder not that, when thou speakest,
Of the weak my heart is weakest.

IV.

As dew beneath the wind of morning,
   As the sea which whirlwinds waken,
As the birds at thunder's warning,
   As aught mute but deeply shaken,
As one who feels an unseen spirit,
Is my heart when thine is near it.

ON THE MEDUSA OF LEONARDO DA VINCI,

IN THE FLORENTINE GALLERY.

I.

It lieth, gazing on the midnight sky,
   Upon the cloudy mountain peak supine;
Below, far lands are seen tremblingly;
   Its horror and its beauty are divine.
Upon its lips and eyelids seems to lie
   Loveliness like a shadow, from which shine,
Fiery and lurid, struggling underneath,
The agonies of anguish and of death.

II.

Yet it is less the horror than the grace
   Which turns the gazer's spirit into stone;
Whereon the lineaments of that dead face
   Are graven, till the characters be grown
Into itself, and thought no more can trace;
   'Tis the melodious hue of beauty thrown
Athwart the darkness and the glare of pain,
Which humanize and harmonize the strain.

III.

And from its head as from one body grow,
   As   grass out of a watery rock,

ON THE MEDUSA.

Hairs which are vipers, and they curl and flow
   And their long tangles in each other lock,
And with unending involutions shew
   Their mailèd radiance, as it were to mock
The torture and the death within, and saw
The solid air with many a ragged jaw.

IV.

And from a stone beside, a poisonous eft
   Peeps idly into those Gorgonian eyes;
Whilst in the air a ghastly bat, bereft
   Of sense, has flitted with a mad surprise
Out of the cave this hideous light had cleft,
   And he comes hastening like a moth that hies
After a taper; and the midnight sky
Flares, a light more dread than obscurity.

V.

'Tis the tempestuous loveliness of terror;
   For from the serpents gleams a brazen glare
Kindled by that inextricable error,
   Which makes a thrilling vapour of the air
Become a   and ever-shifting mirror
   Of all the beauty and the terror there—
A woman's countenance, with serpent locks,
Gazing in death on heaven from those wet rocks.

TO WILLIAM SHELLEY.

(With what truth I may say —
 Roma! Roma! Roma!
Non è più come era prima!)

I.

My lost William, thou in whom
  Some bright spirit lived, and did
That decaying robe consume
  Which its lustre faintly hid,
Here its ashes find a tomb,
  But beneath this pyramid
Thou art not — if a thing divine
Like thee can die, thy funeral shrine
Is thy mother's grief and mine.

II.

Where art thou, my gentle child?
  Let me think thy spirit feeds,
With its life intense and mild,
  The love of living leaves and weeds,
Among these tombs and ruins wild; —
  Let me think that through low seeds
Of the sweet flowers and sunny grass,
Into their hues and scents may pass
A portion ——

THE SENSITIVE PLANT.

PART FIRST.

A Sensitive Plant in a garden grew,
And the young winds fed it with silver dew,
And it opened its fan-like leaves to the light,
And closed them beneath the kisses of night.

And the Spring arose on the garden fair,
Like the Spirit of Love felt every where;
And each flower and herb on Earth's dark breast
Rose from the dreams of its wintry rest.

But none ever trembled and panted with bliss
In the garden, the field, or the wilderness,
Like a doe in the noon-tide with love's sweet want,
As the companionless Sensitive Plant.

The snow-drop, and then the violet,
Arose from the ground with warm rain wet,
And their breath was mixed with fresh odour, sent
From the turf, like the voice and the instrument.

Then the pied wind-flowers and the tulip tall,
And narcissi, the fairest among them all,
Who gaze on their eyes in the stream's recess,
Till they die of their own dear loveliness;

And the Naiad-like lily of the vale,
Whom youth makes so fair and passion so pale,
That the light of its tremulous bells is seen
Through their pavilions of tender green;

And the hyacinth purple, and white, and blue,
Which flung from its bells a sweet peal anew
Of music so delicate, soft, and intense,
It was felt like an odour within the sense;

And the rose like a nymph to the bath addrest,
Which unveiled the depth of her glowing breast,
Till, fold after fold, to the fainting air
The soul of her beauty and love lay bare:

And the wand-like lily, which lifted up,
As a Mænad, its moonlight-coloured cup,
Till the fiery star, which is its eye,
Gazed through clear dew on the tender sky;

And the jessamine faint, and the sweet tuberose,
The sweetest flower for scent that blows;
And all rare blossoms from every clime
Grew in that garden in perfect prime.

And on the stream whose inconstant bosom
Was prankt under boughs of embowering blossom,
With golden and green light, slanting through
Their heaven of many a tangled hue,

Broad water lilies lay tremulously,
And starry river-buds glimmered by,
And around them the soft stream did glide and dance
With a motion of sweet sound and radiance.

And the sinuous paths of lawn and of moss,
Which led through the garden along and across,
Some open at once to the sun and the breeze,
Some lost among bowers of blossoming trees,

Were all paved with daisies and delicate bells
As fair as the fabulous asphodels,
And flowrets which drooping as day drooped too
Fell into pavilions, white, purple, and blue,
To roof the glow-worm from the evening dew.

And from this undefiled Paradise
The flowers (as an infant's awakening eyes
Smile on its mother, whose singing sweet
Can first lull, and at last must awaken it,)

When Heaven's blithe winds had unfolded them,
As mine-lamps enkindle a hidden gem,
Shone smiling to Heaven, and every one
Shared joy in the light of the gentle sun;

For each one was interpenetrated
With the light and the odour its neighbour shed,
Like young lovers whom youth and love make dear
Wrapped and filled by their mutual atmosphere.

But the Sensitive Plant which could give small fruit
Of the love which it felt from the leaf to the root,
Received more than all, it loved more than ever,
Where none wanted but it, could belong to the giver,

For the Sensitive Plant has no bright flower;
Radiance and odour are not its dower;
It loves, even like Love, its deep heart is full,
It desires what it has not, the beautiful!

The light winds which from unsustaining wings
Shed the music of many murmurings;
The beams which dart from many a star
Of the flowers whose hues they bear afar;

The plumèd insects swift and free,
Like golden boats on a sunny sea,
Laden with light and odour, which pass
Over the gleam of the living grass;

The unseen clouds of the dew, which lie
Like fire in the flowers till the sun rides high,
Then wander like spirits among the spheres,
Each cloud faint with the fragrance it bears;

THE SENSITIVE PLANT.

The quivering vapours of dim noontide,
Which like a sea o'er the warm earth glide,
In which every sound, and odour, and beam,
Move, as reeds in a single stream;

Each and all like ministering angels were
For the Sensitive Plant sweet joy to bear,
Whilst the lagging hours of the day went by
Like windless clouds o'er a tender sky.

And when evening descended from heaven above,
And the Earth was all rest, and the air was all love,
And delight, tho' less bright, was far more deep,
And the day's veil fell from the world of sleep,

And the beasts, and the birds, and the insects were drowned
In an ocean of dreams without a sound;
Whose waves never mark, tho' they ever impress
The light sand which paves it, consciousness;

(Only over head the sweet nightingale
Ever sang more sweet as the day might fail,
And snatches of its Elysian chant
Were mixed with the dreams of the Sensitive Plant.)

The Sensitive Plant was the earliest
Up-gathered into the bosom of rest;

THE SENSITIVE PLANT.

A sweet child weary of its delight,
The feeblest and yet the favourite,
Cradled within the embrace of night.

PART SECOND.

There was a Power in this sweet place,
An Eve in this Eden; a ruling grace
Which to the flowers did they waken or dream,
Was as God is to the starry scheme.

A Lady, the wonder of her kind,
Whose form was upborne by a lovely mind
Which, dilating, had moulded her mien and motion
Like a sea-flower unfolded beneath the ocean,

Tended the garden from morn to even:
And the meteors of that sublunar heaven,
Like the lamps of the air when night walks forth,
Laughed round her footsteps up from the Earth!

She had no companion of mortal race,
But her tremulous breath and her flushing face
Told, whilst the morn kissed the sleep from her eyes
That her dreams were less slumber than Paradise:

As if some bright Spirit for her sweet sake
Had deserted heaven while the stars were awake,
As if yet around her he lingering were,
Tho' the veil of daylight concealed him from her.

Her step seemed to pity the grass it prest;
You might hear by the heaving of her breast,
That the coming and going of the wind
Brought pleasure there and left passion behind.

And wherever her airy footstep trod,
Her trailing hair from the grassy sod
Erased its light vestige, with shadowy sweep,
Like a sunny storm o'er the dark green deep.

I doubt not the flowers of that garden sweet
Rejoiced in the sound of her gentle feet;
I doubt not they felt the spirit that came
From her glowing fingers thro' all their frame.

She sprinkled bright water from the stream
On those that were faint with the sunny beam;
And out of the cups of the heavy flowers
She emptied the rain of the thunder showers.

She lifted their heads with her tender hands,
And sustained them with rods and ozier bands;
If the flowers had been her own infants she
Could never have nursed them more tenderly.

THE SENSITIVE PLANT.

And all killing insects and gnawing worms,
And things of obscene and unlovely forms,
She bore in a basket of Indian woof,
Into the rough woods far aloof,

In a basket, of grasses and wild flowers full,
The freshest her gentle hands could pull
For the poor banished insects, whose intent,
Although they did ill, was innocent.

But the bee and the beamlike ephemeris
Whose path is the lightning's, and soft moths that kiss
The sweet lips of the flowers, and harm not, did she
Make her attendant angels be.

And many an antenatal tomb,
Where butterflies dream of the life to come,
She left clinging round the smooth and dark
Edge of the odorous cedar bark.

This fairest creature from earliest spring
Thus moved through the garden ministering
All the sweet season of summer tide,
And ere the first leaf looked brown — she died!

PART THIRD.

Three days the flowers of the garden fair,
Like stars when the moon is awakened, were,
Or the waves of Baiæ, ere luminous
She floats up through the smoke of Vesuvius.

And on the fourth, the Sensitive Plant
Felt the sound of the funeral chaunt,
And the steps of the bearers, heavy and slow,
And the sobs of the mourners deep and low;

The weary sound and the heavy breath,
And the silent motions of passing death,
And the smell, cold, oppressive, and dank,
Sent through the pores of the coffin plank;

The dark grass, and the flowers among the grass,
Were bright with tears as the crowd did pass;
From their sighs the wind caught a mournful tone,
And sate in the pines, and gave groan for groan.

The garden, once fair, became cold and foul,
Like the corpse of her who had been its soul,
Which at first was lovely as if in sleep,
Then slowly changed, till it grew a heap
To make men tremble who never weep.

THE SENSITIVE PLANT.

Swift summer into the autumn flowed,
And frost in the mist of the morning rode,
Though the noonday sun looked clear and bright,
Mocking the spoil of the secret night.

The rose leaves, like flakes of crimson snow,
Paved the turf and the moss below.
The lilies were drooping, and white, and wan,
Like the head and the skin of a dying man.

And Indian plants, of scent and hue
The sweetest that ever were fed on dew,
Leaf after leaf, day after day,
Were massed into the common clay.

And the leaves, brown, yellow, and grey, and red,
And white with the whiteness of what is dead,
Like troops of ghosts on the dry wind past;
Their whistling noise made the birds aghast.

And gusty winds waked the wingèd seeds,
Out of their birthplace of ugly weeds,
Till they clung round many a sweet flower's stem,
Which rotted into the earth with them.

The water-blooms under the rivulet
Fell from the stalks on which they were set;
And the eddies drove them here and there,
As the winds did those of the upper air.

THE SENSITIVE PLANT.

Then the rain came down, and the broken stalks,
Were bent and tangled across the walks;
And the leafless net-work of parasite bowers
Massed into ruin; and all sweet flowers.

Between the time of the wind and the snow,
All loathliest weeds began to grow,
Whose coarse leaves were splashed with many a sp
Like the water-snake's belly and the toad's back.

And thistles, and nettles, and darnels rank,
And the dock, and henbane, and hemlock dank,
Stretched out its long and hollow shank,
And stifled the air till the dead wind stank.

And plants, at whose names the verse feels loath,
Filled the place with a monstrous undergrowth,
Prickly, and pulpous, and blistering, and blue,
Livid, and starred with a lurid dew.

And agarics and fungi, with mildew and mould
Started like mist from the wet ground cold;
Pale, fleshy, as if the decaying dead
With a spirit of growth had been animated!

Their moss rotted off them, flake by flake,
Till the thick stalk stuck like a murderer's stake,
Where rags of loose flesh yet tremble on high,
Infecting the winds that wander by.

Spawn, weeds, and filth, a leprous scum,
Made the running rivulet thick and dumb
And at its outlet flags huge as stakes
Dammed it up with roots knotted like water snakes.

And hour by hour, when the air was still,
The vapours arose which have strength to kill:
At morn they were seen, at noon they were felt,
At night they were darkness no star could melt.

And unctuous meteors from spray to spray
Crept and flitted in broad noon-day
Unseen; every branch on which they alit
By a venomous blight was burned and bit.

The Sensitive Plant like one forbid
Wept, and the tears within each lid
Of its folded leaves which together grew
Were changed to a blight of frozen glue.

For the leaves soon felt, and the branches soon,
By the heavy axe of the blast were hewn;
The sap shrank to the root through every pore
As blood to a heart that will beat no more.

For Winter came: the wind was his whip:
One choppy finger was on his lip:
He had torn the cataracts from the hills
And they clanked at his girdle like manacles;

THE SENSITIVE PLANT.

His breath was a chain which without a sound
The earth, and the air, and the water bound;
He came, fiercely driven, in his chariot-throne
By the tenfold blasts of the arctic zone.

Then the weeds which were forms of living death
Fled from the frost to the earth beneath.
Their decay and sudden flight from frost
Was but like the vanishing of a ghost!

And under the roots of the Sensitive Plant
The moles and the dormice died for want:
The birds dropped stiff from the frozen air
And were caught in the branches naked and bare.

First there came down a thawing rain
And its dull drops froze on the boughs again,
Then there steamed up a freezing dew
Which to the drops of the thaw-rain grew;

And a northern whirlwind, wandering about
Like a wolf that had smelt a dead child out,
Shook the boughs thus laden, and heavy and stiff,
And snapped them off with his rigid griff.

When winter had gone and spring came back
The Sensitive Plant was a leafless wreck;
But the mandrakes, and toadstools, and docks, and
    darnels,
Rose like the dead from their ruined charnels.

CONCLUSION.

Whether the Sensitive Plant, or that
Which within its boughs like a spirit sat
Ere its outward form had known decay,
Now felt this change, I cannot say.

Whether that lady's gentle mind,
No longer with the form combined
Which scattered love, as stars do light,
Found sadness, where it left delight,

I dare not guess; but in this life
Of error, ignorance, and strife,
Where nothing is, but all things seem,
And we the shadows of the dream,

It is a modest creed, and yet
Pleasant if one considers it,
To own that death itself must be,
Like all the rest, a mockery.

That garden sweet, that lady fair,
And all sweet shapes and odours there,
In truth have never past away:
'Tis we, 'tis ours, are changed; not they.

For love, and beauty, and delight,
There is no death nor change: their might
Exceeds our organs, which endure
No light, being themselves obscure.

THE CLOUD.

I BRING fresh showers for the thirsting flowers,
    From the seas and the streams;
I bear light shade for the leaves when laid
    In their noon-day dreams.
From my wings are shaken the dews that waken
    The sweet buds every one,
When rocked to rest on their mother's breast,
    As she dances about the sun.
I wield the flail of the lashing hail,
    And whiten the green plains under,
And then again I dissolve it in rain,
    And laugh as I pass in thunder.

I sift the snow on the mountains below,
    And their great pines groan aghast;
And all the night 'tis my pillow white,
    While I sleep in the arms of the blast.
Sublime on the towers of my skiey bowers,
    Lightning my pilot sits,
In a cavern under is fettered the thunder,
    It struggles and howls at fits;

THE CLOUD.

Over earth and ocean, with gentle motion,
    This pilot is guiding me,
Lured by the love of the genii that move
    In the depths of the purple sea;
Over the rills, and the crags, and the hills,
    Over the lakes and the plains,
Wherever he dream, under mountain or stream,
    The Spirit he loves remains;
And I all the while bask in heaven's blue smile,
    Whilst he is dissolving in rains.

The sanguine sunrise, with his meteor eyes,
    And his burning plumes outspread,
Leaps on the back of my sailing rack,
    When the morning star shines dead,
As on the jag of a mountain crag,
    Which an earthquake rocks and swings,
An eagle alit one moment may sit
    In the light of its golden wings.
And when sunset may breathe, from the lit sea beneath,
    Its ardours of rest and of love,
And the crimson pall of eve may fall
    From the depth of heaven above,
With wings folded I rest, on mine airy nest,
    As still as a brooding dove.

THE CLOUD.

That orbèd maiden with white fire laden,
    Whom mortals call the moon,
Glides glimmering o'er my fleece-like floor,
    By the midnight breezes strewn;
And wherever the beat of her unseen feet,
    Which only the angels hear,
May have broken the woof of my tent's thin roof,
    The stars peep behind her and peer;
And I laugh to see them whirl and flee,
    Like a swarm of golden bees,
When I widen the rent in my wind-built tent,
    Till the calm rivers, lakes, and seas,
Like strips of the sky fallen through me on high,
    Are each paved with the moon and these.

I bind the sun's throne with a burning zone,
    And the moon's with a girdle of pearl;
The volcanoes are dim, and the stars reel and swim,
    When the whirlwinds my banner unfurl.
From cape to cape, with a bridge-like shape,
    Over a torrent sea,
Sunbeam-proof, I hang like a roof,
    The mountains its columns be.
The triumphal arch through which I march
    With hurricane, fire, and snow,

THE CLOUD.

When the powers of the air are chained to my chair,
    Is the million-coloured bow ;
The sphere-fire above its soft colours wove,
    While the moist earth was laughing below.

I am the daughter of earth and water,
    And the nursling of the sky ;
I pass through the pores of the ocean and shores ;
    I change, but I cannot die.
For after the rain when with never a stain,
    The pavilion of heaven is bare,
And the winds and sunbeams with their convex gleams,
    Build up the blue dome of air,
I silently laugh at my own cenotaph,
    And out of the caverns of rain,
Like a child from the womb, like a ghost from the tomb,
    I arise and unbuild it again.

TO A SKYLARK.

Hail to thee, blithe spirit !
   Bird thou never wert,
That from heaven, or near it,
   Pourest thy full heart
In profuse strains of unpremeditated art.

   Higher still and higher
     From the earth thou springest
   Like a cloud of fire;
     The blue deep thou wingest,
And singing still dost soar, and soaring ever singest.

   In the golden lightning
     Of the sunken sun,
   O'er which clouds are brightning,
     Thou dost float and run;
Like an unbodied joy whose race is just begun.

   The pale purple even
     Melts around thy flight;
   Like a star of heaven,
     In the broad day-light
Thou art unseen, but yet I hear thy shrill delight.

TO A SKYLARK.

Keen as are the arrows
 Of that silver sphere,
Whose intense lamp narrows
 In the white dawn clear,
Until we hardly see, we feel that it is there.

All the earth and air
 With thy voice is loud,
As, when night is bare,
 From one lonely cloud
The moon rains out her beams, and heaven is overflowed.

What thou art we know not;
 What is most like thee?
From rainbow clouds there flow not
 Drops so bright to see,
As from thy presence showers a rain of melody.

Like a poet hidden
 In the light of thought,
Singing hymns unbidden,
 Till the world is wrought
To sympathy with hopes and fears it heeded not:

Like a high-born maiden
 In a palace tower,
Soothing her love-laden
 Soul in secret hour
With music sweet as love, which overflows her bower:

TO A SKYLARK.

Like a glow-worm golden
   In a dell of dew,
Scattering unbeholden
   Its aërial hue
Among the flowers and grass, which screen it from the view:

Like a rose embowered
   In its own green leaves,
By warm winds deflowered,
   Till the scent it gives
Makes faint with too much sweet these heavy-wing thieves:

Sound of vernal showers
   On the twinkling grass,
Rain-awakened flowers,
   All that ever was
Joyous, and clear, and fresh, thy music doth surpass

Teach us, sprite or bird,
   What sweet thoughts are thine:
I have never heard
   Praise of love or wine
That panted forth a flood of rapture so divine.

Chorus Hymenæal,
   Or triumphal chaunt,

TO A SKYLARK.

Matched with thine would be all
    But an empty vaunt,
A thing wherein we feel there is some hidden want.

What objects are the fountains
    Of thy happy strain?
What fields, or waves, or mountains?
    What shapes of sky or plain?
What love of thine own kind? what ignorance of pain?

With thy clear keen joyance
    Languor cannot be:
Shadow of annoyance
    Never came near thee:
Thou lovest; but ne'er knew love's sad satiety.

Waking or asleep,
    Thou of death must deem
Things more true and deep
    Than we mortals dream,
Or how could thy notes flow in such a crystal stream?

We look before and after,
    And pine for what is not:
Our sincerest laughter
    With some pain is fraught;
Our sweetest songs are those that tell of saddest thought.

TO A SKYLARK.

Yet if we could scorn
    Hate, and pride, and fear;
If we were things born
    Not to shed a tear,
I know not how thy joy we ever should come near.

Better than all measures
    Of delightful sound,
Better than all treasures
    That in books are found,
Thy skill to poet were, thou scorner of the ground!

Teach me half the gladness
    That thy brain must know,
Such harmonious madness
    From my lips would flow,
The world should listen then, as I am listening now.

ODE TO LIBERTY.

Yet, Freedom, yet thy banner torn but flying,
Streams like a thunder-storm against the wind.
                                        BYRON.

I.

A GLORIOUS people vibrated again:
  The lightning of the nations, Liberty,
From heart to heart, from tower to tower, o'er Spain,
  Scattering contagious fire into the sky,
Gleamed. My soul spurned the chains of its dismay,
      And, in the rapid plumes of song,
      Clothed itself, sublime and strong;
As a young eagle soars the morning clouds among,
  Hovering in verse o'er its accustomed prey;
    Till from its station in the heaven of fame
  The Spirit's whirlwind rapt it, and the ray
    Of the remotest sphere of living flame
Which paves the void was from behind it flung,
  As foam from a ship's swiftness, when there came
  A voice out of the deep: I will record the same.

II.

The Sun and the serenest Moon sprang forth:
  The burning stars of the abyss were hurled

ODE TO LIBERTY.

Into the depths of heaven. The dædal earth,
  That island in the ocean of the world,
Hung in its cloud of all-sustaining air:
    But this divinest universe
    Was yet a chaos and a curse,
For thou wert not: but power from worst produ
    worse,
  The spirit of the beasts was kindled there,
    And of the birds, and of the watery forms,
  And there was war among them, and despair
    Within them, raging without truce or terms:
The bosom of their violated nurse
  Groaned, for beasts warred on beasts, and worm
    worms,
  And men on men; each heart was as a hell of sto

III.

Man, the imperial shape, then multiplied
  His generations under the pavilion
Of the Sun's throne: palace and pyramid,
  Temple and prison, to many a swarming million,
Were, as to mountain-wolves their ragged caves.
    This human living multitude
    Was savage, cunning, blind, and rude,
For thou wert not; but o'er the populous solitude,
  Like one fierce cloud over a waste of waves
    Hung Tyranny; beneath, sate deified

ODE TO LIBERTY.

The sister-pest, congregator of slaves;
 Into the shadow of her pinions wide
Anarchs and priests who feed on gold and blood,
 Till with the stain their inmost souls are dyed,
 Drove the astonished herds of men from every side.

IV.

The nodding promontories, and blue isles,
 And cloud-like mountains, and dividuous waves
Of Greece, basked glorious in the open smiles
 Of favoring heaven: from their enchanted caves
Prophetic echoes flung dim melody.
  On the unapprehensive wild
  The vine, the corn, the olive mild,
Grew savage yet, to human use unreconciled;
 And, like unfolded flowers beneath the sea,
  Like the man's thought dark in the infant's brain,
 Like aught that is which wraps what is to be,
  Art's deathless dreams lay veiled by many a vein
Of Parian stone; and yet a speechless child,
 Verse murmured, and Philosophy did strain
 Her lidless eyes for thee; when o'er the Ægean main

V.

Athens arose: a city such as vision
 Builds from the purple crags and silver towers

ODE TO LIBERTY.

Of battlemented cloud, as in derision
  Of kingliest masonry: the ocean-floors
Pave it; the evening sky pavilions it;
    Its portals are inhabited
    By thunder-zonèd winds, each head
Within its cloudy wings with sunfire garlanded,
  A divine work! Athens diviner yet
    Gleamed with its crest of columns, on the will
  Of man, as on a mount of diamond, set;
    For thou wert, and thine all-creative skill
Peopled with forms that mock the eternal dead
  In marble immortality, that hill
  Which was thine earliest throne and latest oracle.

VI.

Within the surface of Time's fleeting river
  Its wrinkled image lies, as then it lay
Immovably unquiet, and for ever
  It trembles, but it cannot pass away!
The voices of thy bards and sages thunder
    With an earth-awakening blast
    Through the caverns of the past;
Religion veils her eyes; Oppression shrinks aghast:
  A wingèd sound of joy, and love, and wonder,
    Which soars where Expectation never flew,
  Rending the veil of space and time asunder!
    One ocean feeds the clouds, and streams, and dew;

One sun illumines heaven; one spirit vast
  With life and love makes chaos ever new,
  As Athens doth the world with thy delight renew.

VII.

Then Rome was, and from thy deep bosom fairest,
  Like a wolf-cub from a Cadmæan Mænad,
She drew the milk of greatness, though thy dearest
  From that Elysian food was yet unweanèd;
And many a deed of terrible uprightness
    By thy sweet love was sanctified;
    And in thy smile, and by thy side,
Saintly Camillus lived, and firm Atilius died.
  But when tears stained thy robe of vestal whiteness,
    And gold profaned thy capitolian throne,
  Thou didst desert, with spirit-wingèd lightness,
    The senate of the tyrants: they sunk prone
Slaves of one tyrant: Palatinus sighed
  Faint echoes of Ionian song; that tone
  Thou didst delay to hear, lamenting to disown.

VIII.

From what Hyrcanian glen or frozen hill,
  Or piny promontory of the Arctic main,
Or utmost islet inaccessible,
  Didst thou lament the ruin of thy reign,

ODE TO LIBERTY.

Teaching the woods and waves, and desart rocks,
    And every Naiad's ice-cold urn,
    To talk in echoes sad and stern,
Of that sublimest lore which man had dared unlearn?
    For neither didst thou watch the wizard flocks
      Of the Scald's dreams, nor haunt the Druid's sleep
    What if the tears rained through thy shattered locks
      Were quickly dried? for thou didst groan, not weep.
When from its sea of death to kill and burn,
    The Galilean serpent forth did creep,
    And made thy world an undistinguishable heap.

IX.

A thousand years the Earth cried, Where art thou?
    And then the shadow of thy coming fell
On Saxon Alfred's olive-cinctured brow:
    And many a warrior-peopled citadel,
Like rocks which fire lifts out of the flat deep,
      Arose in sacred Italy,
      Frowning o'er the tempestuous sea
Of kings, and priests, and slaves, in tower-crowned
      majesty;
    That multitudinous anarchy did sweep,
      And burst around their walls, like idle foam,
    Whilst from the human spirit's deepest deep
      Strange melody with love and awe struck dumb
Dissonant arms; and Art, which cannot die,

With divine wand traced on our earthly home
Fit imagery to pave heaven's everlasting dome.

X.

Thou huntress swifter than the Moon! thou terror
   Of the world's wolves! thou bearer of the quiver,
Whose sunlike shafts pierce tempest-wingèd Error,
   As light may pierce the clouds when they dissever
In the calm regions of the orient day!
      Luther caught thy wakening glance,
      Like lightning, from his leaden lance
Reflected, it dissolved the visions of the trance
   In which, as in a tomb, the nations lay;
     And England's prophets hailed thee as their queen,
   In songs whose music cannot pass away,
     Though it must flow for ever: not unseen
Before the spirit-sighted countenance
   Of Milton didst thou pass, from the sad scene
   Beyond whose night he saw, with a dejected mien.

XI.

The eager hours and unreluctant years
   As on a dawn-illumined mountain stood,
Trampling to silence their loud hopes and fears,
   Darkening each other with their multitude,
And cried aloud, Liberty! Indignation

ODE TO LIBERTY.

 Answered Pity from her cave ;
 Death grew pale within the grave,
And Desolation howled to the destroyer, Save !
 When like heaven's sun girt by the exhalation
  Of its own glorious light, thou didst arise,
 Chasing thy foes from nation unto nation
  Like shadows : as if day had cloven the skies
At dreaming midnight o'er the western wave,
 Men started, staggering with a glad surprise,-
Under the lightnings of thine unfamiliar eyes.

XII.

Thou heaven of earth ! what spells could pall thee then,
 In ominous eclipse ? a thousand years
Bred from the slime of deep oppression's den,
 Dyed all thy liquid light with blood and tears,
Till thy sweet stars could weep the stain away ;
  How like Bacchanals of blood
  Round France, the ghastly vintage, stood
Destruction's sceptred slaves, and Folly's mitred brood !
 When one, like them, but mightier far than they,
  The Anarch of thine own bewildered powers
 Rose : armies mingled in obscure array,
  Like clouds with clouds, darkening the sacred bowers
Of serene heaven· He, by the past pursued,

Rests with those dead, but unforgotten hours,
Whose ghosts scare victor kings in their ancestral
  towers.

XIII.

England yet sleeps: was she not called of old?
  Spain calls her now, as with its thrilling thunder
Vesuvius wakens Ætna, and the cold
  Snow-crags by its reply are cloven in sunder:
O'er the lit waves every Æolian isle
    From Pithecusa to Pelorus
    Howls, and leaps, and glares in chorus:
They cry, Be dim; ye lamps of heaven suspended o'er
  us.
  Her chains are threads of gold, she need but smile
    And they dissolve; but Spain's were links of steel,
  Till bit to dust by virtue's keenest file.
    Twins of a single destiny! appeal
To the eternal years enthroned before us,
  In the dim West; impress us from a seal,
  All ye have thought and done! Time cannot dare
    conceal.

XIV.

Tomb of Arminius! render up thy dead,
  Till, like a standard from a watch-tower's staff,

His soul may stream over the tyrant's head;
 Thy victory shall be his epitaph,
Wild Bacchanal of truth's mysterious wine,
  King-deluded Germany,
  His dead spirit lives in thee.
Why do we fear or hope? thou art already free!
 And thou, lost Paradise of this divine
  And glorious world! thou flowery wilderness!
 Thou island of eternity! thou shrine
  Where desolation clothed with loveliness,
Worships the thing thou wert! O Italy,
 Gather thy blood into thy heart; repress
 The beasts who make their dens thy sacred palaces.

XV.

O, that the free would stamp the impious name
 Of KING into the dust! or write it there,
So that this blot upon the page of fame
 Were as a serpent's path, which the light air
Erases, and the flat sands close behind!
  Ye the oracle have heard:
  Lift the victory-flashing sword,
And cut the snaky knots of this foul gordian word,
 Which weak itself as stubble, yet can bind
  Into a mass, irrefragably firm,
 The axes and the rods which awe mankind;
  The sound has poison in it, 'tis the sperm

Of what makes life foul, cankerous, and abhorred;
  Disdain not thou, at thine appointed term,
  To set thine armèd heel on this reluctant worm.

XVI.

O, that the wise from their bright minds would kindle
  Such lamps within the dome of this dim world,
That the pale name of PRIEST might shrink and dwindle
  Into the hell from which it first was hurled,
A scoff of impious pride from fiends impure;
    Till human thoughts might kneel alone
    Each before the judgment-throne
Of its own aweless soul, or of the power unknown!
  O, that the words which make the thoughts obscure
    From which they spring, as clouds of glimmering
      dew
  From a white lake blot heaven's blue portraiture,
    Were stript of their thin masks and various hue
And frowns and smiles and splendours not their own,
  Till in the nakedness of false and true
  They stand before their Lord, each to receive its due.

XVII.

He who taught man to vanquish whatsoever
  Can be between the cradle and the grave
Crowned him the King of Life. O vain endeavour!
  If on his own high will a willing slave,

He has enthroned the oppression and the oppressor.
    What if earth can clothe and feed
    Amplest millions at their need,
And power in thought be as the tree within the seed?
    O, what if Art, an ardent intercessor,
      Driving on fiery wings to Nature's throne,
    Checks the great mother stooping to caress her,
      And cries: Give me, thy child, dominion
Over all height and depth? if Life can breed
    New wants, and wealth from those who toil and groan
    Rend of thy gifts and hers a thousand fold for one.

XVIII.

Come Thou, but lead out of the inmost cave
    Of man's deep spirit, as the morning-star
Beckons the Sun from the Eoan wave,
    Wisdom. I hear the pennons of her car
Self-moving, like cloud charioted by flame;
      Comes she not, and come ye not,
      Rulers of eternal thought,
To judge, with solemn truth, life's ill-apportioned lot?
    Blind Love, and equal Justice, and the Fame
      Of what has been, the Hope of what will be?
    O, Liberty! if such could be thy name
      Wert thou disjoined from these, or they from thee:
If thine or theirs were treasures to be bought

By blood or tears, have not the wise and free
  Wept tears, and blood like tears? The solemn
    harmony

XIX.

Paused, and the spirit of that mighty singing
  To its abyss was suddenly withdrawn;
Then, as a wild swan, when sublimely winging
  Its path athwart the thunder-smoke of dawn,
Sinks headlong through the aërial golden light
    On the heavy sounding plain,
    When the bolt has pierced its brain;
As summer clouds dissolve, unburthened of their rain;
  As a far taper fades with fading night,
    As a brief insect dies with dying day,
  My song, its pinions disarrayed of might,
    Drooped; o'er it closed the echoes far away
Of the great voice which did its flight sustain,
  As waves which lately paved his watery way
    Hiss round a drowner's head in their tempestuous
      play.

EPIPSYCHIDION.

Sweet Spirit! Sister of that orphan one,
Whose empire is the name thou weepest on,
In my heart's temple I suspend to thee
These votive wreaths of withered memory.

Poor captive bird! who, from thy narrow cage,
Pourest such music, that it might assuage
The rugged hearts of those who prisoned thee,
Were they not deaf to all sweet melody;
This song shall be thy rose: its petals pale
Are dead, indeed, my adored Nightingale!
But soft and fragrant is the faded blossom,
And it has no thorn left to wound thy bosom.

High, spirit-wingèd Heart! who dost for ever
Beat thine unfeeling bars with vain endeavour,
Till those bright plumes of thought, in which arrayed
It over-soared this low and worldly shade,
Lie shattered; and thy panting, wounded breast
Stains with dear blood its unmaternal nest!

I weep vain tears: blood would less bitter be,
Yet poured forth gladlier, could it profit thee.

Seraph of Heaven! too gentle to be human,
Veiling beneath that radiant form of Woman
All that is insupportable in thee
Of light, and love, and immortality!
Sweet Benediction in the eternal Curse!
Veiled Glory of this lampless Universe!
Thou Moon beyond the clouds! Thou living Form
Among the Dead! Thou Star above the Storm!
Thou Wonder, and thou Beauty, and thou Terror!
Thou Harmony of Nature's art! Thou Mirror
In whom, as in the splendour of the Sun,
All shapes look glorious which thou gazest on!
Aye, even the dim words which obscure thee now
Flash, lightning-like, with unaccustomed glow;
I pray thee that thou blot from this sad song
All of its much mortality and wrong,
With those clear drops, which start like sacred dew
From the twin lights thy sweet soul darkens through,
Weeping, till sorrow becomes ecstasy:
Then smile on it, so that it may not die.

I never thought before my death to see
Youth's vision thus made perfect. Emily,

I love thee; though the world by no thin name
Will hide that love, from its unvalued shame.
Would we two had been twins of the same mother!
Or, that the name my heart lent to another
Could be a sister's bond for her and thee,
Blending two beams of one eternity!
Yet were one lawful and the other true,
These names, though dear, could paint not, as is due,
How beyond refuge I am thine. Ah me!
I am not thine: I am a part of *thee*.

Sweet Lamp! my moth-like Muse has burnt its wings;
Or, like a dying swan who soars and sings,
Young Love should teach Time, in his own grey style,
All that thou art. Art thou not void of guile,
A lovely soul formed to be blest and bless?
A well of sealed and secret happiness,
Whose waters like blithe light and music are,
Vanquishing dissonance and gloom? A Star
Which moves not in the moving Heavens, alone?
A smile amid dark frowns? a gentle tone
Amid rude voices? a belovèd light?
A Solitude, a Refuge, a Delight?
A Lute, which those whom love has taught to play
Make music on, to soothe the roughest day
And lull fond grief asleep? a buried treasure?
A cradle of young thoughts of wingless pleasure?

A violet-shrouded grave of Woe?—I measure
The world of fancies, seeking one like thee,
And find—alas! mine own infirmity.

    She met me, Stranger, upon life's rough way,
And lured me towards sweet Death; as Night by Day,
Winter by Spring, or Sorrow by swift Hope,
Led into light, life, peace. An antelope,
In the suspended impulse of its lightness,
Were less ætherially light: the brightness
Of her divinest presence trembles through
Her limbs, as underneath a cloud of dew
Embodied in the windless Heaven of June
Amid the splendour-wingèd stars, the Moon
Burns, inextinguishably beautiful:
And from her lips, as from a hyacinth full
Of honey-dew, a liquid murmur drops,
Killing the sense with passion; sweet as stops
Of planetary music heard in trance.
In her mild lights the starry spirits dance,
The sun-beams of those wells which ever leap
Under the lightnings of the soul—too deep
For the brief fathom-line of thought or sense.
The glory of her being, issuing thence,
Stains the dead, blank, cold air with a warm shade
Of unentangled intermixture, made

By Love, of light and motion: one intense
Diffusion, one serene Omnipresence,
Whose flowing outlines mingle in their flowing
Around her cheeks and utmost fingers glowing
With the unintermitted blood, which there
Quivers, (as in a fleece of snow-like air
The crimson pulse of living morning quiver,)
Continuously prolonged, and ending never,
Till they are lost, and in that Beauty furled
Which penetrates and clasps and fills the world;
Scarce visible from extreme loveliness.
Warm fragrance seems to fall from her light dress,
And her loose hair; and where some heavy tress
The air of her own speed has disentwined,
The sweetness seems to satiate the faint wind;
And in the soul a wild odour is felt,
Beyond the sense, like fiery dews that melt
Into the bosom of a frozen bud.——
See where she stands! a mortal shape indued
With love and life and light and deity,
And motion which may change but cannot die;
An image of some bright Eternity;
A shadow of some golden dream; a Splendour
Leaving the third sphere pilotless; a tender
Reflection of the eternal Moon of Love
Under whose motions life's dull billows move;

A Metaphor of Spring and Youth and Morning;
A Vision like incarnate April, warning,
With smiles and tears, Frost the Anatomy
Into his summer grave.

     Ah, woe is me!
What have I dared? where am I lifted? how
Shall I descend, and perish not? I know
That Love makes all things equal: I have heard
By mine own heart this joyous truth averred:
The spirit of the worm beneath the sod
In love and worship, blends itself with God.

 Spouse! Sister! Angel! Pilot of the Fate
Whose course has been so starless! O too late
Belovèd! O too soon adored, by me!
For in the fields of immortality
My spirit should at first have worshipped thine,
A divine presence in a place divine;
Or should have moved beside it on this earth,
A shadow of that substance, from its birth;
But not as now: - - - I love thee; yes, I feel
That on the fountain of my heart a seal
Is set, to keep its waters pure and bright
For thee, since in those *tears* thou hast delight.
We — are we not formed, as notes of music are,
For one another, though dissimilar;

Such difference without discord, as can make
Those sweetest sounds, in which all spirits shake
As trembling leaves in a continuous air?

Thy wisdom speaks in me, and bids me dare
Beacon the rocks on which high hearts are wreckt.
I never was attached to that great sect,
Whose doctrine is, that each one should select
Out of the crowd a mistress or a friend,
And all the rest, though fair and wise, commend
To cold oblivion, though it is in the code
Of modern morals, and the beaten road
Which those poor slaves with weary footsteps tread,
Who travel to their home among the dead
By the broad highway of the world, and so
With one chained friend, perhaps a jealous foe,
The dreariest and the longest journey go.

True Love in this differs from gold and clay,
That to divide is not to take away.
Love is like understanding, that grows bright,
Gazing on many truths; 'tis like thy light,
Imagination! which from earth and sky,
And from the depths of human phantasy,
As from a thousand prisms and mirrors, fills
The Universe with glorious beams, and kills

Error, the worm, with many a sun-like arrow
Of its reverberated lightning. Narrow
The heart that loves, the brain that contemplates,
The life that wears, the spirit that creates
One object, and one form, and builds thereby
A sepulchre for its eternity.

Mind from its object differs most in this:
Evil from good; misery from happiness;
The baser from the nobler; the impure
And frail, from what is clear and must endure.
If you divide suffering and dross, you may
Diminish till it is consumed away;
If you divide pleasure and love and thought,
Each part exceeds the whole; and we know not
How much, while any yet remains unshared,
Of pleasure may be gained, of sorrow spared:
This truth is that deep well, whence sages draw
The unenvied light of hope; the eternal law
By which those live, to whom this world of life
Is as a garden ravaged, and whose strife
Tills for the promise of a later birth
The wilderness of this Elysian earth.

There was a Being whom my spirit oft
Met on its visioned wanderings, far aloft,

In the clear golden prime of my youth's dawn,
Upon the fairy isles of sunny lawn,
Amid the enchanted mountains, and the caves
Of divine sleep, and on the air-like waves
Of wonder-level dream, whose tremulous floor
Paved her light steps;—on an imagined shore,
Under the grey beak of some promontory
She met me, robed in such exceeding glory,
That I beheld her not. In solitudes
Her voice came to me through the whispering woods,
And from the fountains, and the odours deep
Of flowers, which, like lips murmuring in their sleep
Of the sweet kisses which had lulled them there,
Breathed but of *her* to the enamoured air;
And from the breezes whether low or loud,
And from the rain of every passing cloud,
And from the singing of the summer-birds,
And from all sounds, all silence. In the words
Of antique verse and high romance,— in form,
Sound, colour—in whatever checks that Storm
Which with the shattered present chokes the past;
And in that best philosophy, whose taste
Makes this cold common hell, our life, a doom
As glorious as a fiery martyrdom;
Her Spirit was the harmony of truth.—

Then, from the caverns of my dreamy youth
I sprang, as one sandalled with plumes of fire,
And towards the loadstar of my one desire,
I flitted, like a dizzy moth, whose flight
Is as a dead leaf's in the owlet light,
When it would seek in Hesper's setting sphere
A radiant death, a fiery sepulchre,
As if it were a lamp of earthly flame.—
But She, whom prayers or tears then could not tame,
Past, like a God throned on a wingèd planet,
Whose burning plumes to tenfold swiftness fan it,
Into the dreary cone of our life's shade;
And as a man with mighty loss dismayed,
I would have followed, though the grave between
Yawned like a gulf whose spectres are unseen:
When a voice said:—" O Thou of hearts the weakest,
" The phantom is beside thee whom thou seekest."
Then I—"where?" the world's echo answered
  "where!"
And in that silence, and in my despair,
I questioned every tongueless wind that flew
Over my tower of mourning, if it knew
Whither 'twas fled, this soul out of my soul;
And murmured names and spells which have controul
Over the sightless tyrants of our fate;
But neither prayer nor verse could dissipate
The night which closed on her; nor uncreate

That world within this Chaos, mine and me,
Of which she was the veiled Divinity,
The world I say of thoughts that worshipped her:
And therefore I went forth, with hope and fear
And every gentle passion sick to death,
Feeding my course with expectation's breath,
Into the wintry forest of our life;
And struggling through its error with vain strife,
And stumbling in my weakness and my haste,
And half bewildered by new forms, I past
Seeking among those untaught foresters
If I could find one form resembling hers,
In which she might have masked herself from me.
There,—One, whose voice was venomed melody
Sate by a well, under blue night-shade bowers;
The breath of her false mouth was like faint flowers,
Her touch was as electric poison,—flame
Out of her looks into my vitals came,
And from her living cheeks and bosom flew
A killing air, which pierced like honey-dew
Into the core of my green heart, and lay
Upon its leaves; until, as hair grown grey
O'er a young brow, they hid its unblown prime
With ruins of unseasonable time.

In many mortal forms I rashly sought
The shadow of that idol of my thought.

And some were fair — but beauty dies away:
Others were wise — but honeyed words betray:
And One was true — oh! why not true to me?
Then, as a hunted deer that could not flee,
I turned upon my thoughts, and stood at bay,
Wounded and weak and panting; the cold day
Trembled, for pity of my strife and pain.
When, like a noon-day dawn, there shone again
Deliverance. One stood on my path who seemed
As like the glorious shape which I had dreamed,
As is the Moon, whose changes ever run
Into themselves, to the eternal Sun;
The cold chaste Moon, the Queen of Heaven's bright
    isles,
Who makes all beautiful on which she smiles,
That wandering shrine of soft yet icy flame
Which ever is transformed, yet still the same,
And warms not but illumines. Young and fair
As the descended Spirit of that sphere,
She hid me, as the Moon may hide the night
From its own darkness, until all was bright
Between the Heaven and Earth of my calm mind,
And, as a cloud charioted by the wind,
She led me to a cave in that wild place,
And sate beside me, with her downward face
Illumining my slumbers, like the Moon
Waxing and waning o'er Endymion.

And I was laid asleep, spirit and limb,
And all my being became bright or dim
As the Moon's image in a summer sea,
According as she smiled or frowned on me;
And there I lay, within a chaste cold bed:
Alas, I then was nor alive nor dead:—
For at her silver voice came Death and Life,
Unmindful each of their accustomed strife,
Masked like twin babes, a sister and a brother,
The wandering hopes of one abandoned mother,
And through the cavern without wings they flew,
And cried "Away, he is not of our crew."
I wept, and though it be a dream, I weep.

What storms then shook the ocean of my sleep,
Blotting that Moon, whose pale and waning lips
Then shrank as in the sickness of eclipse;—
And how my soul was as a lampless sea,
And who was then its Tempest; and when She,
The Planet of that hour, was quenched, what frost
Crept o'er those waters, till from coast to coast
The moving billows of my being fell .
Into a death of ice, immovable;—
And then—what earthquakes made it gape and split,
The white Moon smiling all the while on it,
These words conceal:—If not, each word would be
The key of staunchless tears. Weep not for me!

At length, into the obscure Forest came
The Vision I had sought through grief and shame.
Athwart that wintry wilderness of thorns
Flashed from her motion splendour like the Morn's,
And from her presence life was radiated
Through the grey earth and branches bare and dead;
So that her way was paved, and roofed above
With flowers as soft as thoughts of budding love;
And music from her respiration spread
Like light,—all other sounds were penetrated
By the small, still, sweet spirit of that sound,
So that the savage winds hung mute around;
And odours warm and fresh fell from her hair
Dissolving the dull cold in the frore air:
Soft as an Incarnation of the Sun,
When light is changed to love, this glorious One
Floated into the cavern where I lay,
And called my Spirit, and the dreaming clay
Was lifted by the thing that dreamed below
As smoke by fire, and in her beauty's glow
I stood, and felt the dawn of my long night
Was penetrating me with living light:
I knew it was the Vision veiled from me
So many years—that it was Emily.

Twin Spheres of light who rule this passive Earth,
This world of love, this *me;* and into birth

Awaken all its fruits and flowers, and dart
Magnetic might into its central heart;
And lift its billows and its mists, and guide
By everlasting laws, each wind and tide
To its fit cloud, and its appointed cave;
And lull its storms, each in the craggy grave
Which was its cradle, luring to faint bowers
The armies of the rain-bow-wingèd showers;
And, as those married lights, which from the towers
Of Heaven look forth and fold the wandering globe
In liquid sleep and splendour, as a robe;
And all their many-mingled influence blend,
If equal, yet unlike, to one sweet end;—
So ye, bright regents, with alternate sway
Govern my sphere of being, night and day!
Thou, not disdaining even a borrowed might;
Thou, not eclipsing a remoter light;
And, through the shadow of the seasons three,
From Spring to Autumn's sere maturity,
Light it into the Winter of the tomb,
Where it may ripen to a brighter bloom.
Thou too, O Comet beautiful and fierce,
Who drew the heart of this frail Universe
Towards thine own; till, wreckt in that convulsion,
Alternating attraction and repulsion,
Thine went astray and that was rent in twain;
Oh, float into our azure heaven again!

Be there love's folding-star at thy return;
The living Sun will feed thee from its urn
Of golden fire; the Moon will veil her horn
In thy last smiles; adoring Even and Morn
Will worship thee with incense of calm breath
And lights and shadows; as the star of Death
And Birth is worshipped by those sisters wild
Called Hope and Fear — upon the heart are piled
Their offerings, — of this sacrifice divine
A World shall be the altar.

                      Lady mine,
Scorn not these flowers of thought, the fading birth
Which from its heart of hearts that plant puts forth
Whose fruit, made perfect by thy sunny eyes,
Will be as of the trees of Paradise.

  The day is come, and thou wilt fly with me.
To whatsoe'er of dull mortality
Is mine, remain a vestal sister still;
To the intense, the deep, the imperishable,
Not mine but me, henceforth be thou united
Even as a bride, delighting and delighted.
The hour is come :---the destined Star has risen
Which shall descend upon a vacant prison.
The walls are high, the gates are strong, thick set
The sentinels --- but true love never yet

Was thus constrained : it overleaps all fence :
Like lightning, with invisible violence
Piercing its continents; like Heaven's free breath,
Which he who grasps can hold not; liker Death,
Who rides upon a thought, and makes his way
Through temple, tower, and palace, and the array
Of arms: more strength has Love than he or they;
For it can burst his charnel, and make free
The limbs in chains, the heart in agony,
The soul in dust and chaos.

      Emily,
A ship is floating in the harbour now,
A wind is hovering o'er the mountain's brow;
There is a path on the sea's azure floor,
No keel has ever ploughed that path before;
The halcyons brood around the foamless isles;
The treacherous Ocean has forsworn its wiles;
The merry mariners are bold and free :
Say, my heart's sister, wilt thou sail with me?
Our bark is as an albatross, whose nest
Is a far Eden of the purple East;
And we between her wings will sit, while Night
And Day, and Storm, and Calm, pursue their flight,
Our ministers, along the boundless Sea,
Treading each other's heels, unheededly.

It is an isle under Ionian skies,
Beautiful as a wreck of Paradise,
And, for the harbours are not safe and good,
This land would have remained a solitude
But for some pastoral people native there,
Who from the Elysian, clear, and golden air
Draw the last spirit of the age of gold,
Simple and spirited; innocent and bold.
The blue Ægean girds this chosen home,
With ever-changing sound and light and foam,
Kissing the sifted sands, and caverns hoar;
And all the winds wandering along the shore
Undulate with the undulating tide:
There are thick woods where sylvan forms abide;
And many a fountain, rivulet, and pond,
As clear as elemental diamond,
Or serene morning air; and far beyond,
The mossy tracks made by the goats and deer
(Which the rough shepherd treads but once a year,)
Pierce into glades, caverns, and bowers, and halls
Built round with ivy, which the waterfalls
Illumining, with sound that never fails
Accompany the noon-day nightingales;
And all the place is peopled with sweet airs;
The light clear element which the isle wears
Is heavy with the scent of lemon-flowers,
Which floats like mist laden with unseen showers,

And falls upon the eye-lids like faint sleep;
And from the moss violets and jonquils peep,
And dart their arrowy odour through the brain
'Till you might faint with that delicious pain.
And every motion, odour, beam, and tone,
With that deep music is in unison:
Which is a soul within the soul - - - they seem
Like echoes of an antenatal dream. —
It is an isle 'twixt Heaven, Air, Earth, and Sea,
Cradled, and hung in clear tranquillity;
Bright as that wandering Eden Lucifer,
Washed by the soft blue Oceans of young air.
It is a favoured place. Famine or Blight,
Pestilence, War and Earthquake, never light
Upon its mountain-peaks; blind vultures, they
Sail onward far upon their fatal way:
The wingèd storms, chaunting their thunder-psalm
To other lands, leave azure chasms of calm
Over this isle, or weep themselves in dew,
From which its fields and woods ever renew
Their green and golden immortality.
And from the sea there rise, and from the sky
There fall, clear exhalations, soft and bright,
Veil after veil, each hiding some delight,
Which Sun or Moon or zephyr draw aside,
Till the isle's beauty, like a naked bride

Glowing at once with love and loveliness,
Blushes and trembles at its own excess:
Yet, like a buried lamp, a Soul no less
Burns in the heart of this delicious isle,
An atom of th' Eternal, whose own smile
Unfolds itself, and may be felt, not seen
O'er the grey rocks, blue waves, and forests green,
Filling their bare and void interstices.—
But the chief marvel of the wilderness
Is a lone dwelling, built by whom or how
None of the rustic island-people know:
'Tis not a tower of strength, though with its height
It overtops the woods; but, for delight,
Some wise and tender Ocean-King, ere crime
Had been invented, in the world's young prime,
Reared it, a wonder of that simple time,
An envy of the isles, a pleasure-house
Made sacred to his sister and his spouse.
It scarce seems now a wreck of human art,
But, as it were Titanic; in the heart
Of Earth having assumed its form, then grown
Out of the mountains, from the living stone,
Lifting itself in caverns light and high:
For all the antique and learnèd imagery
Has been erased, and in the place of it
The ivy and the wild-vine interknit

The volumes of their many twining stems;
Parasite flowers illume with dewy gems
The lampless halls, and when they fade, the sky
Peeps through their winter-woof of tracery
With Moon-light patches, or star atoms keen,
Or fragments of the day's intense serene;—
Working mosaic on their Parian floors.
And, day and night, aloof, from the high towers
And terraces, the Earth and Ocean seem
To sleep in one another's arms, and dream
Of waves, flowers, clouds, woods, rocks, and all that
Read in their smiles, and call reality.

This isle and house are mine, and I have vowed
Thee to be lady of the solitude.---
And I have fitted up some chambers there
Looking towards the golden Eastern air,
And level with the living winds, which flow
Like waves above the living waves below.---
I have sent books and music there, and all
Those instruments with which high spirits call
The future from its cradle, and the past
Out of its grave, and make the present last
In thoughts and joys which sleep, but cannot die,
Folded within their own eternity.
Our simple life wants little, and true taste
Hires not the pale drudge Luxury, to waste

The scene it would adorn, and therefore still,
Nature with all her children, haunts the hill.
The ring-dove, in the embowering ivy, yet
Keeps up her love-lament, and the owls flit
Round the evening tower, and the young stars glance
Between the quick bats in their twilight dance;
The spotted deer bask in the fresh moon-light
Before our gate, and the slow, silent night
Is measured by the pants of their calm sleep.
Be this our home in life, and when years heap
Their withered hours, like leaves, on our decay,
Let us become the over-hanging day,
The living soul of this Elysian isle,
Conscious, inseparable, one. Meanwhile
We two will rise, and sit, and walk together,
Under the roof of blue Ionian weather,
And wander in the meadows, or ascend
The mossy mountains, where the blue heavens bend
With lightest winds, to touch their paramour;
Or linger, where the pebble-paven shore,
Under the quick, faint kisses of the sea
Trembles and sparkles as with ecstasy, - - -
Possessing and possest by all that is
Within that calm circumference of bliss,
And by each other, till to love and live
Be one : - - - or, at the noontide hour, arrive

Where some old cavern hoar seems yet to keep
The moonlight of the expired night asleep,
Through which the awakened day can never peep;
A veil for our seclusion, close as Night's,
Where secure sleep may kill thine innocent lights;
Sleep, the fresh dew of languid love, the rain
Whose drops quench kisses till they burn again.
And we will talk, until thought's melody
Become too sweet for utterance, and it die
In words, to live again in looks, which dart
With thrilling tone into the voiceless heart,
Harmonizing silence without a sound.
Our breath shall intermix, our bosoms bound,
And our veins beat together; and our lips
With other eloquence than words, eclipse
The soul that burns between them, and the wells
Which boil under our being's inmost cells,
The fountains of our deepest life, shall be
Confused in passion's golden purity,
As mountain springs under the morning Sun.
We shall become the same, we shall be one
Spirit within two frames, oh! wherefore two?
One passion in twin-hearts, which grows and grew,
Till like two meteors of expanding flame,
Those spheres instinct with it become the same,
Touch, mingle, are transfigured; ever still
Burning, yet ever inconsumable:

In one another's substance finding food,
Like flames too pure and light and unimbued
To nourish their bright lives with baser prey,
Which point to Heaven and cannot pass away:
One hope within two wills, one will beneath
Two overshadowing minds, one life, one death,
One Heaven, one Hell, one immortality,
And one annihilation. Woe is me!
The wingèd words on which my soul would pierce
Into the height of love's rare Universe,
Are chains of lead around its flight of fire.---
I pant, I sink, I tremble, I expire!

Weak Verses, go, kneel at your Sovereign's feet,
And say:—"We are the masters of thy slave;
"What wouldest thou with us and ours and thine?"
Then call your sisters from Oblivion's cave,
All singing loud: "Love's very pain is sweet,
"But its reward is in the world divine
"Which, if not here, it builds beyond the grave."
So shall ye live when I am there. Then haste
Over the hearts of men, until ye meet
Marina, Vanna, Primus, and the rest,
And bid them love each other and be blest:
And leave the troop which errs, and which reproves,
And come and be my guest,---for I am Love's.

"DEATH IS HERE AND DEATH IS THERE."

DEATH.

I.

Death is here and death is there,
Death is busy everywhere,
All around, within, beneath,
Above is death — and we are death.

II.

Death has set his mark and seal
On all we are and all we feel,
On all we know and all we fear,

* * * *

III.

First our pleasures die — and then
Our hopes, and then our fears — and when
These are dead, the debt is due,
Dust claims dust — and we die too.

IV.

All things that we love and cherish,
Like ourselves must fade and perish,
Such is our rude mortal lot —
Love itself would, did they not.

"THE WARM SUN IS FAILING."

AUTUMN.

A DIRGE.

I.

The warm sun is failing, the bleak wind is wailing,
The bare boughs are sighing, the pale flowers are dying,
      And the year
On the earth her death-bed, in a shroud of leaves dead,
      Is lying.
    Come, months, come away,
    From November to May,
    In your saddest array;
    Follow the bier
    Of the dead cold year,
And like dim shadows watch by her sepulchre.

II.

The chill rain is falling, the nipt worm is crawling,
The rivers are swelling, the thunder is knelling
      For the year;
The blithe swallows are flown, and the lizards each gone
      To his dwelling;
    Come, months, come away;
    Put on white, black, and grey;
    Let your light sisters play —
    Ye, follow the bier
    Of the dead cold year,
And make her grave green with tear on tear.

LETTER TO MARIA GISBORNE.

Leghorn, July 1, 1820.

The spider spreads her webs, whether she be
In poet's tower, cellar, or barn, or tree;
The silkworm in the dark green mulberry leaves
His winding sheet and cradle ever weaves;
So I, a thing whom moralists call worm,
Sit spinning still round this decaying form,
From the fine threads of rare and subtle thought —
No net of words in garish colours wrought
To catch the idle buzzers of the day —
But a soft cell, where when that fades away,
Memory may clothe in wings my living name
And feed it with the asphodels of fame,
Which in those hearts which must remember me
Grow, making love an immortality.

Whoever should behold me now, I wist,
Would think I were a mighty mechanist,
Bent with sublime Archimedean art
To breathe a soul into the iron heart
Of some machine portentous, or strange gin,
Which by the force of figured spells might win
Its way over the sea, and sport therein;

For round the walls are hung dread engines, such
As Vulcan never wrought for Jove to clutch
Ixion or the Titan : — or the quick
Wit of that man of God, St. Dominic,
To convince Atheist, Turk or Heretic,
Or those in philanthropic council met,
Who thought to pay some interest for the debt
They owed to Jesus Christ for their salvation,
By giving a faint foretaste of damnation
To Shakespeare, Sidney, Spenser and the rest
Who made our land an island of the blest,
When lamp-like Spain, who now relumes her fire
On Freedom's hearth, grew dim with Empire : —
With thumbscrews, wheels, with tooth and spike and
    jag,
Which fishers found under the utmost crag
Of Cornwall and the storm-encompassed isles,
Where to the sky the rude sea rarely smiles
Unless in treacherous wrath, as on the morn
When the exulting elements in scorn
Satiated with destroyed destruction, lay
Sleeping in beauty on their mangled prey,
As panthers sleep ; — and other strange and dread
Magical forms the brick floor overspread ——
Proteus transformed to metal did not make
More figures, or more strange ; nor did he take

Such shapes of unintelligible brass,
Or heap himself in such a horrid mass
Of tin and iron not to be understood;
And forms of unimaginable wood,
To puzzle Tubal Cain and all his brood:
Great screws, and cones, and wheels, and grooved
    blocks,
The elements of what will stand the shocks
Of wave and wind and time. — Upon the table
More knacks and quips there be than I am able
To catalogize in this verse of mine: —
A pretty bowl of wood — not full of wine,
But quicksilver; that dew which the gnomes drink
When at their subterranean toil they swink,
Pledging the demons of the earthquake, who
Reply to them in lava — cry halloo!
And call out to the cities o'er their head, —
Roofs, towers and shrines, the dying and the dead,
Crash through the chinks of earth — and then all quaff
Another rouse, and hold their sides and laugh.
This quicksilver no gnome has drunk — within
The walnut bowl it lies, vinèd and thin,
In colour like the wake of light that stains
The Tuscan deep, when from the moist moon rains
The inmost shower of it's white fire — the breeze
Is still — blue heaven smiles over the pale seas.

And in this bowl of quicksilver — for I
Yield to the impulse of an infancy
Outlasting manhood — I have made to float
A rude idealism of a paper boat: —
A hollow screw with cogs — Henry will know
The thing I mean and laugh at me, — if so
He fears not I should do more mischief. — Next
Lie bills and calculations much perplext,
With steam-boats, frigates, and machinery quaint
Traced over them in blue and yellow paint.
Then comes a range of mathematical
Instruments, for plans nautical and statical;
A heap of rosin, a queer broken glass
With ink in it; — a china cup that was
What it will never be again, I think,
A thing from which sweet lips were wont to drink
The liquor doctors rail at — and which I
Will quaff in spite of them — and when we die
We'll toss up who died first of drinking tea,
And cry out, — heads or tails? where'er we be.
Near that a dusty paint box, some odd hooks,
A half-burnt match, an ivory block, three books,
Where conic sections, spherics, logarithms,
To great Laplace, from Saunderson and Sims,
Lie heaped in their harmonious disarray
Of figures, — disentangle them who may.

Baron de Tott's Memoirs beside them lie,
And some odd volumes of old chemistry.
Near those a most inexplicable thing,
With lead in the middle — I'm conjecturing
How to make Henry understand; but no —
I'll leave, as Spenser says, with many mo,
This secret in the pregnant womb of time,
Too vast a matter for so weak a rhyme.

And here like some weird Archimage sit I,
Plotting dark spells, and devilish enginery,
The self-impelling steam-wheels of the mind
Which pump up oaths from clergymen, and grind
The gentle spirit of our meek reviews
Into a powdery foam of salt abuse,
Ruffling the ocean of their self-content; —
I sit — and smile or sigh as is my bent,
But not for them — Libeccio rushes round
With an inconstant and an idle sound,
I heed him more than them — the thunder-smoke
Is gathering on the mountains, like a cloak
Folded athwart their shoulders broad and bare;
The ripe corn under the undulating air
Undulates like an ocean; — and the vines
Are trembling wide in all their trellised lines —
The murmur of the awakening sea doth fill
The empty pauses of the blast; — the hill

Looks hoary through the white electric rain,
And from the glens beyond, in sullen strain,
The interrupted thunder howls; above
One chasm of heaven smiles, like the eye of Love
On the unquiet world;—while such things are,
How could one worth your friendship heed the war
Of worms? the shriek of the world's carrion jays,
Their censure, or their wonder, or their praise?

You are not here! the quaint witch Memory sees
In vacant chairs, your absent images,
And points where once you sat, and now should be
But are not.—I demand if ever we
Shall meet as then we met;—and she replies,
Veiling in awe her second-sighted eyes;
" I know the past alone — but summon home
" My sister Hope,—she speaks of all to come."
But I, an old diviner, who knew well
Every false verse of that sweet oracle,
Turned to the sad enchantress once again,
And sought a respite from my gentle pain,
In citing every passage o'er and o'er
Of our communion — how on the sea shore
We watched the ocean and the sky together,
Under the roof of blue Italian weather;
How I ran home through last year's thunder-storm,
And felt the transverse lightning linger warm

Upon my cheek — and how we often made
Feasts for each other, where good will outweighed
The frugal luxury of our country cheer,
As well it might, were it less firm and clear
Than ours must ever be ; — and how we spun
A shroud of talk to hide us from the sun
Of this familiar life, which seems to be
But is not, — or is but quaint mockery
Of all we would believe, and sadly blame
The jarring and inexplicable frame
Of this wrong world : — and then anatomize
The purposes and thoughts of men whose eyes
Were closed in distant years ; — or widely guess
The issue of the earth's great business,
When we shall be as we no longer are —
Like babbling gossips safe, who hear the war
Of winds, and sigh, but tremble not ; — or how
You listened to some interrupted flow
Of visionary rhyme, — in joy and pain
Struck from the inmost fountains of my brain,
With little skill perhaps ; — or how we sought
Those deepest wells of passion or of thought
Wrought by wise poets in the waste of years,
Staining their sacred waters with our tears ;
Quenching a thirst ever to be renewed !
Or how I, wisest lady ! then indued

The language of a land which now is free,
And winged with thoughts of truth and majesty,
Flits round the tyrant's sceptre like a cloud,
And bursts the peopled prisons, and cries aloud,
'My name is Legion!'—that majestic tongue
Which Calderon over the desart flung
Of ages and of nations; and which found
An echo in our hearts, and with the sound
Startled oblivion;—thou wert then to me
As is a nurse—when inarticulately
A child would talk as it's grown parents do.
If living winds the rapid clouds pursue,
If hawks chase doves through the ætherial way,
Huntsmen the innocent deer, and beasts their prey,
Why should not we rouse with the spirit's blast
Out of the forest of the pathless past
These recollected pleasures?

       You are now
In London, that great sea, whose ebb and flow
At once is deaf and loud, and on the shore
Vomits its wrecks, and still howls on for more.
Yet in its depth what treasures! You will see
That which was Godwin,—greater none than he
Though fallen—and fallen on evil times—to stand
Among the spirits of our age and land,

Before the dread tribunal of *to come*
The foremost,— while Rebuke cowers pale and du
You will see Coleridge — he who sits obscure
In the exceeding lustre, and the pure
Intense irradiation of a mind,
Which, with its own internal lightning blind,
Flags wearily through darkness and despair —
A cloud-encircled meteor of the air,
A hooded eagle among blinking owls. ——
You will see Hunt — one of those happy souls
Which are the salt of the earth, and without whom
This world would smell like what it is — a tomb;
Who is, what others seem; his room no doubt
Is still adorned by many a cast from Shout,
With graceful flowers tastefully placed about;
And coronals of bay from ribbons hung,
And brighter wreaths in neat disorder flung;
The gifts of the most learn'd among some dozens
Of female friends, sisters-in-law and cousins.
And there is he with his eternal puns,
Which beat the dullest brain for smiles, like duns
Thundering for money at a poet's door;
Alas! it is no use to say, "I'm poor!"
Or oft in graver mood, when he will look
Things wiser than were ever read in book,
Except in Shakespeare's wisest tenderness. —
You will see Hogg, — and I cannot express

's virtues,—though I know that they are great,
cause he locks, then barricades the gate
thin which they inhabit;—of his wit
d wisdom, you'll cry out when you are bit.
is a pearl within an oyster shell,
e of the richest of the deep;—and there
English Peacock with his mountain fair
rned into a Flamingo;—that shy bird
at gleams i' the Indian air—have you not heard
hen a man marries, dies, or turns Hindoo,
s best friends hear no more of him?—but you
ll see him, and will like him too, I hope,
ith the milk-white Snowdonian Antelope
atched with this cameleopard—his fine wit
akes such a wound, the knife is lost in it;
strain too learnèd for a shallow age,
o wise for selfish bigots; let his page
hich charms the chosen spirits of the time,
ld itself up for the serener clime
years to come, and find it's recompense
that just expectation.—Wit and sense,
rtue and human knowledge; all that might
ake this dull world a business of delight,
e all combined in Horace Smith.—And these,
ith some exceptions, which I need not teaze
ur patience by descanting on,—are all
u and I know in London.

                              I recall
My thoughts, and bid you look upon the night.
As water does a sponge, so the moonlight
Fills the void, hollow, universal air —
What see you? — unpavilioned heaven is fair
Whether the moon, into her chamber gone,
Leaves midnight to the golden stars, or wan
Climbs with diminished beams the azure steep;
Or whether clouds sail o'er the inverse deep,
Piloted by the many-wandering blast,
And the rare stars rush through them dim and
    fast: ——
All this is beautiful in every land.——
But what see you beside? — a shabby stand
Of Hackney coaches — a brick house or wall
Fencing some lonely court, white with the scrawl
Of our unhappy politics; — or worse —
A wretched woman reeling by, whose curse
Mixed with the watchman's, partner of her trade,
You must accept in place of serenade —
Or yellow-haired Pollonia murmuring
To Henry, some unutterable thing.
I see a chaos of green leaves and fruit
Built round dark caverns, even to the root
Of the living stems that feed them — in whose bc
There sleep in their dark dew the folded flowers;
Beyond, the surface of the unsickled corn

LETTER TO MARIA GISBORNE.

Trembles not in the slumbering air, and borne
In circles quaint, and ever changing dance,
Like wingèd stars the fire-flies flash and glance,
Pale in the open moonshine, but each one
Under the dark trees seems a little sun,
A meteor tamed ; a fixed star gone astray
From the silver regions of the milky way ; —
Afar the Contadino's song is heard,
Rude, but made sweet by distance — and a bird
Which cannot be the Nightingale, and yet
I know none else that sings so sweet as it
At this late hour ; — and then all is still ——
Now Italy or London, which you will !

Next winter you must pass with me ; I'll have
My house by that time turned into a grave
Of dead despondence and low-thoughted care,
And all the dreams which our tormentors are ;
Oh ! that Hunt, Hogg, Peacock and Smith were there
With every thing belonging to them fair ! —
We will have books, Spanish, Italian, Greek ;
And ask one week to make another week
As like his father, as I'm unlike mine,
Which is not his fault, as you may divine.
Though we eat little flesh and drink no wine,
Yet let's be merry : we'll have tea and toast ;
Custards for supper, and an endless host

Of syllabubs and jellies and mince-pies,
And other such lady-like luxuries, —
Feasting on which we will philosophize!
And we'll have fires out of the Grand Duke's wood,
To thaw the six weeks' winter in our blood.
And then we'll talk ; — what shall we talk about?
Oh! there are themes enough for many a bout
Of thought-entangled descant ; — as to nerves —
With cones and parallelograms and curves,
I've sworn to strangle them if once they dare
To bother me — when you are with me there.
And they shall never more sip laudanum,
From Helicon or Himeros ; — well, come,
And in despite of God and of the devil,
We'll make our friendly philosophic revel
Outlast the leafless time ; till buds and flowers
Warn the obscure inevitable hours,
Sweet meeting by sad parting to renew ; —
"Tomorrow to fresh woods and pastures new."

THE WITCH OF ATLAS.

I.

Before those cruel Twins, whom at one birth
   Incestuous Change bore to her father Time,
Error and Truth, had hunted from the Earth
   All those bright natures which adorned its prime,
And left us nothing to believe in, worth
   The pains of putting into learnèd rhyme,
A lady-witch there lived on Atlas' mountain
Within a cavern, by a secret fountain.

II.

Her mother was one of the Atlantides:
   The all-beholding Sun had ne'er beholden
In his wide voyage o'er continents and seas
   So fair a creature, as she lay enfolden
In the warm shadow of her loveliness;—
   He kissed her with his beams, and made all golden
The chamber of grey rock in which she lay—
She, in that dream of joy, dissolved away.

III.

'Tis said, she first was changed into a vapour,
   And then into a cloud, such clouds as flit,
Like splendour-wingèd moths about a taper,
   Round the red west when the sun dies in it:
And then into a meteor, such as caper
   On hill-tops when the moon is in a fit:
Then, into one of those mysterious stars
Which hide themselves between the Earth and Mars.

IV.

Ten times the Mother of the Months had bent
   Her bow beside the folding-star, and bidden
With that bright sign the billows to indent
   The sea-deserted sand — like children chidden,
At her command they ever came and went —
   Since in that cave a dewy splendour hidden
Took shape and motion: with the living form
Of this embodied Power, the cave grew warm.

V.

A lovely lady garmented in light
   From her own beauty — deep her eyes, as are
Two openings of unfathomable night
   Seen through a Temple's cloven roof — her hair

Dark — the dim brain whirls dizzy with delight,
  Picturing her form; her soft smiles shone afar,
And her low voice was heard like love, and drew
All living things towards this wonder new.

VI.

And first the spotted cameleopard came,
  And then the wise and fearless elephant;
Then the sly serpent, in the golden flame
  Of his own volumes intervolved; — all gaunt
And sanguine beasts her gentle looks made tame.
  They drank before her at her sacred fount;
And every beast of beating heart grew bold,
Such gentleness and power even to behold.

VII.

The brinded lioness led forth her young,
  That she might teach them how they should forego
Their inborn thirst of death; the pard unstrung
  His sinews at her feet, and sought to know
With looks whose motions spoke without a tongue
  How he might be as gentle as the doe.
The magic circle of her voice and eyes
All savage natures did imparadise.

VIII.

And old Silenus, shaking a green stick
  Of lilies, and the wood-gods in a crew
Came, blithe, as in the olive copses thick
  Cicadæ are, drunk with the noonday dew:
And Dryope and Faunus followed quick,
  Teazing the God to sing them something new;
Till in this cave they found the lady lone,
Sitting upon a seat of emerald stone.

IX.

And universal Pan, 'tis said, was there,
  And though none saw him,—through the adamant
Of the deep mountains, through the trackless air,
  And through those living spirits, like a want
He past out of his everlasting lair
  Where the quick heart of the great world doth pant,
And felt that wondrous lady all alone,—
And she felt him, upon her emerald throne.

X.

And every nymph of stream and spreading tree,
  And every shepherdess of Ocean's flocks,
Who drives her white waves over the green sea,
  And Ocean with the brine on his grey locks,

And quaint Priapus with his company,
　All came, much wondering how the enwombèd rocks
Could have brought forth so beautiful a birth;—
Her love subdued their wonder and their mirth.

XI.

The herdsmen and the mountain maidens came,
　And the rude kings of pastoral Garamant—
Their spirits shook within them, as a flame
　Stirred by the air under a cavern gaunt:
Pigmies, and Polyphemes, by many a name,
　Centaurs and Satyrs, and such shapes as haunt
Wet clefts,—and lumps neither alive nor dead,
Dog-headed, bosom-eyed, and bird-footed.

XII.

For she was beautiful—her beauty made
　The bright world dim, and every thing beside
Seemed like the fleeting image of a shade:
　No thought of living spirit could abide,
Which to her looks had ever been betrayed,
　On any object in the world so wide,
On any hope within the circling skies,
But on her form, and in her inmost eyes.

XIII.

Which when the lady knew, she took her spindle
  And twined three threads of fleecy mist, and three
Long lines of light, such as the dawn may kindle
  The clouds and waves and mountains with; and s]
As many star-beams, ere their lamps could dwindle
  In the belated moon, wound skilfully;
And with these threads a subtle veil she wove —
A shadow for the splendour of her love.

XIV.

The deep recesses of her odorous dwelling
  Were stored with magic treasures — sounds of air,
Which had the power all spirits of compelling,
  Folded in cells of crystal silence there;
Such as we hear in youth, and think the feeling
  Will never die — yet ere we are aware,
The feeling and the sound are fled and gone,
And the regret they leave remains alone.

XV.

And there lay Visions swift, and sweet, and quaint,
  Each in its thin sheath, like a chrysalis,
Some eager to burst forth, some weak and faint
  With the soft burthen of intensest bliss;

It was its work to bear to many a saint
   Whose heart adores the shrine which holiest is,
Even Love's : — and others white, green, grey and black,
And of all shapes — and each was at her beck.

XVI.

And odours in a kind of aviary
   Of ever-blooming Eden-trees she kept,
Clipt in a floating net, a love-sick Fairy
   Had woven from dew-beams while the moon yet slept;
As bats at the wired window of a dairy,
   They beat their vans; and each was an adept,
When loosed and missioned, making wings of winds,
To stir sweet thoughts or sad, in destined minds.

XVII.

And liquors clear and sweet, whose healthful might
   Could medicine the sick soul to happy sleep,
And change eternal death into a night
   Of glorious dreams — or if eyes needs must weep,
Could make their tears all wonder and delight,
   She in her crystal vials did closely keep:
If men could drink of those clear vials, 'tis said
The living were not envied of the dead.

XVIII.

Her cave was stored with scrolls of strange device,
  The works of some Saturnian Archimage,
Which taught the expiations at whose price
  Men from the Gods might win that happy age
Too lightly lost, redeeming native vice;
  And which might quench the Earth-consuming rage
Of gold and blood — till men should live and move
Harmonious as the sacred stars above;

XIX.

And how all things that seem untameable,
  Not to be checked and not to be confined,
Obey the spells of wisdom's wizard skill;
  Time, earth and fire — the ocean and the wind,
And all their shapes — and man's imperial will;
  And other scrolls whose writings did unbind
The inmost lore of Love — let the profane
Tremble to ask what secrets they contain.

XX.

And wondrous works of substances unknown,
  To which the enchantment of her father's power
Had changed those ragged blocks of savage stone,
  Were heaped in the recesses of her bower;

Carved lamps and chalices, and vials which shone
  In their own golden beams — each like a flower,
Out of whose depth a fire-fly shakes his light
Under a cypress in a starless night.

XXI.

At first she lived alone in this wild home,
  And her own thoughts were each a minister,
Clothing themselves, or with the ocean foam,
  Or with the wind, or with the speed of fire,
To work whatever purposes might come
  Into her mind; such power her mighty Sire
Had girt them with, whether to fly or run,
Through all the regions which he shines upon.

XXII.

The Ocean-nymphs and Hamadryades,
  Oreads and Naiads, with long weedy locks,
Offered to do her bidding through the seas,
  Under the earth, and in the hollow rocks,
And far beneath the matted roots of trees,
  And in the knarlèd heart of stubborn oaks,
So they might live for ever in the light
Of her sweet presence — each a satellite.

XXIII.

"This may not be," the wizard maid replied;
  "The fountains where the Naiades bedew
"Their shining hair, at length are drained and dried;
  "The solid oaks forget their strength, and strew
"Their latest leaf upon the mountains wide;
  "The boundless ocean like a drop of dew
"Will be consumed — the stubborn centre must
"Be scattered, like a cloud of summer dust.

XXIV.

"And ye with them will perish, one by one; —
  "If I must sigh to think that this shall be,
"If I must weep when the surviving Sun
  "Shall smile on your decay — Oh, ask not me
"To love you till your little race is run;
  "I cannot die as ye must — over me
"Your leaves shall glance — the streams in which ye dwell
"Shall be my paths henceforth, and so — farewell!" —

XXV.

She spoke and wept: — the dark and azure well
  Sparkled beneath the shower of her bright tears,
And every little circlet where they fell
  Flung to the cavern-roof inconstant spheres

And intertangled lines of light: — a knell
  Of sobbing voices came upon her ears
From those departing Forms, o'er the serene
Of the white streams and of the forest green.

XXVI.

All day the wizard lady sate aloof,
  Spelling out scrolls of dread antiquity,
Under the cavern's fountain-lighted roof;
  Or broidering the pictured poesy
Of some high tale upon her growing woof,
  Which the sweet splendour of her smiles could dye
In hues outshining Heaven — and ever she
Added some grace to the wrought poesy.

XXVII.

While on her hearth lay blazing many a piece
  Of sandal wood, rare gums and cinnamon;
Men scarcely know how beautiful fire is —
  Each flame of it is as a precious stone
Dissolved in ever-moving light, and this
  Belongs to each and all who gaze upon.
The Witch beheld it not, for in her hand
She held a woof that dimmed the burning brand.

XXVIII.

'This lady never slept, but lay in trance
    All night within the fountain — as in sleep.
Its emerald crags glowed in her beauty's glance;
    Through the green splendour of the water deep
She saw the constellations reel and dance
    Like fire-flies — and withal did ever keep
The tenour of her contemplations calm,
With open eyes, closed feet and folded palm.

XXIX.

And when the whirlwinds and the clouds descended
    From the white pinnacles of that cold hill,
She past at dewfall to a space extended,
    Where in a lawn of flowering asphodel
Amid a wood of pines and cedars blended,
    There yawned an inextinguishable well
Of crimson fire — full even to the brim,
And overflowing all the margin trim.

XXX.

Within the which she lay when the fierce war
    Of wintry winds shook that innocuous liquor
In many a mimic moon and bearded star
    O'er woods and lawns; — the serpent heard it fli

In sleep, and dreaming still, he crept afar—
And when the windless snow descended thicker
Than autumn leaves, she watched it as it came
Melt on the surface of the level flame.

XXXI.

She had a Boat, which some say Vulcan wrought
    For Venus, as the chariot of her star;
But it was found too feeble to be fraught
    With all the ardours in that sphere which are,
And so she sold it, and Apollo bought
    And gave it to this daughter: from a car
Changed to the fairest and the lightest boat
Which ever upon mortal stream did float.

XXXII.

And others say, that, when but three hours old,
    The first-born Love out of his cradle leapt,
And clove dun Chaos with his wings of gold,
    And like an Horticultural adept,
Stole a strange seed, and wrapt it up in mould,
    And sowed it in his mother's star, and kept
Watering it all the summer with sweet dew,
And with his wings fanning it as it grew.

XXXIII.

The plant grew strong and green, the snowy flower
    Fell, and the long and gourd-like fruit began
To turn the light and dew by inward power
    To its own substance; woven tracery ran
Of light firm texture, ribbed and branching, o'er
    The solid rind, like a leaf's veinèd fan —
Of which Love scooped this boat — and with soft motion
Piloted it round the circumfluous ocean.

XXXIV.

This boat she moored upon her fount, and lit
    A living spirit within all its frame,
Breathing the soul of swiftness into it.
    Couched on the fountain like a panther tame,
One of the twain at Evan's feet that sit —
    Or as on Vesta's sceptre a swift flame —
Or on blind Homer's heart a wingèd thought, —
In joyous expectation lay the boat.

XXXV.

Then by strange art she kneaded fire and snow
    Together, tempering the repugnant mass
With liquid love — all things together grow
    Through which the harmony of love can pass;

And a fair Shape out of her hands did flow —
  A living Image, which did far surpass
In beauty that bright shape of vital stone
Which drew the heart out of Pygmalion.

XXXVI.

A sexless thing it was, and in its growth
  It seemed to have developed no defect
Of either sex, yet all the grace of both, —
  In gentleness and strength its limbs were decked;
The bosom swelled lightly with its full youth,
  The countenance was such as might select
Some artist that his skill should never die,
Imaging forth such perfect purity.

XXXVII.

From its smooth shoulders hung two rapid wings,
  Fit to have borne it to the seventh sphere,
Tipt with the speed of liquid lightnings,
  Dyed in the ardours of the atmosphere:
She led her creature to the boiling springs
  Where the light boat was moored, and said: "Sit here!"
And pointed to the prow, and took her seat
Beside the rudder, with opposing feet.

XXXVIII.

And down the streams which clove those mountains
   Around their inland islets, and amid
The panther-peopled forests, whose shade cast
   Darkness and odours, and a pleasure hid
In melancholy gloom, the pinnace past;
   By many a star-surrounded pyramid
Of icy crag cleaving the purple sky,
And caverns yawning round unfathomably.

XXXIX.

The silver noon into that winding dell,
   With slanted gleam athwart the forest tops,
Tempered like golden evening, feebly fell;
   A green and glowing light, like that which drops
From folded lilies in which glow-worms dwell,
   When earth over her face night's mantle wraps;
Between the severed mountains lay on high
Over the stream, a narrow rift of sky.

XL.

And ever as she went, the Image lay
   With folded wings and unawakened eyes;
And o'er its gentle countenance did play
   The busy dreams, as thick as summer flies,

Chasing the rapid smiles that would not stay,
   And drinking the warm tears, and the sweet sighs
Inhaling, which, with busy murmur vain,
They had aroused from that full heart and brain.

XLI.

And ever down the prone vale, like a cloud
   Upon a stream of wind, the pinnace went:
Now lingering on the pools, in which abode
   The calm and darkness of the deep content
In which they paused; now o'er the shallow road
   Of white and dancing waters, all besprent
With sand and polished pebbles:—mortal boat
In such a shallow rapid could not float.

XLII.

And down the earthquaking cataracts which shiver
   Their snow-like waters into golden air,
Or under chasms unfathomable ever
   Sepulchre them, till in their rage they tear
A subterranean portal for the river,
   It fled—the circling sunbows did upbear
Its fall down the hoar precipice of spray,
Lighting it far upon its lampless way.

XLIII.

And when the wizard lady would ascend
  The labyrinths of some many-winding vale,
Which to the inmost mountain upward tend —
  She called "Hermaphroditus!" — and the pale
And heavy hue which slumber could extend
  Over its lips and eyes, as on the gale
A rapid shadow from a slope of grass,
Into the darkness of the stream did pass.

XLIV.

And it unfurled its heaven-coloured pinions,
  With stars of fire spotting the stream below;
And from above into the Sun's dominions
  Flinging a glory, like the golden glow
In which spring clothes her emerald-wingèd minions,
  All interwoven with fine feathery snow
And moonlight splendour of intensest rime,
With which frost paints the pines in winter time.

XLV.

And then it winnowed the Elysian air
  Which ever hung about that lady bright,
With its ætherial vans — and speeding there,
  Like a star up the torrent of the night,

Or a swift eagle in the morning glare
  Breasting the whirlwind with impetuous flight,
The pinnace, oared by those enchanted wings,
Clove the fierce streams towards their upper springs.

XLVI.

The water flashed like sunlight by the prow
  Of a noon-wandering meteor flung to Heaven;
The still air seemed as if its waves did flow
  In tempest down the mountains; loosely driven
The lady's radiant hair streamed to and fro:
  Beneath, the billows having vainly striven
Indignant and impetuous, roared to feel
The swift and steady motion of the keel.

XLVII.

Or, when the weary moon was in the wane,
  Or in the noon of interlunar night,
The lady-witch in visions could not chain
  Her spirit; but sailed forth under the light
Of shooting stars, and bade extend amain
  Its storm-outspeeding wings, the Hermaphrodite;
She to the Austral waters took her way,
Beyond the fabulous Thamondocana.

XLVIII.

Where, like a meadow which no scythe has shaven,
   Which rain could never bend, or whirl-blast shake,
With the Antarctic constellations paven,
   Canopus and his crew, lay the Austral lake —
There she would build herself a windless haven
   Out of the clouds whose moving turrets make
The bastions of the storm, when through the sky
The spirits of the tempest thundered by.

XLIX.

A haven beneath whose translucent floor
   The tremulous stars sparkled unfathomably,
And around which the solid vapours hoar,
   Based on the level waters, to the sky
Lifted their dreadful crags, and like a shore
   Of wintry mountains, inaccessibly
Hemmed in with rifts and precipices grey,
And hanging crags, many a cove and bay.

L.

And whilst the outer lake beneath the lash
   Of the wind's scourge, foamed like a wounded thing
And the incessant hail with stony clash
   Ploughed up the waters, and the flagging wing

Of the roused cormorant in the lightning flash
   Looked like the wreck of some wind-wandering
Fragment of inky thunder-smoke — this haven
Was as a gem to copy Heaven engraven.

LI.

On which that lady played her many pranks,
   Circling the image of a shooting star,
Even as a tiger on Hydaspes' banks
   Outspeeds the antelopes which speediest are,
In her light boat; and many quips and cranks
   She played upon the water, till the car
Of the late moon, like a sick matron wan,
To journey from the misty east began.

LII.

And then she called out of the hollow turrets
   Of those high clouds, white, golden and vermilion,
The armies of her ministering spirits —
   In mighty legions, million after million,
They came, each troop emblazoning its merits
   On meteor flags; and many a proud pavilion
Of the intertexture of the atmosphere
They pitched upon the plain of the calm mere.

THE WITCH OF ATLAS.

LIII.

They framed the imperial tent of their great Queen
    Of woven exhalations, underlaid
With lambent lightning-fire, as may be seen
    A dome of thin and open ivory inlaid
With crimson silk — cressets from the serene
    Hung there, and on the water for her tread
A tapestry of fleece-like mist was strewn,
Dyed in the beams of the ascending moon.

LIV.

And on a throne o'erlaid with starlight, caught
    Upon those wandering isles of aëry dew,
Which highest shoals of mountain shipwreck not,
    She sate, and heard all that had happened new
Between the earth and moon, since they had brought
    The last intelligence — and now she grew
Pale as that moon, lost in the watery night —
And now she wept, and now she laughed outright.

LV.

These were tame pleasures; she would often climb
    The steepest ladder of the crudded rack
Up to some beakèd cape of cloud sublime,
    And like Arion on the dolphin's back

Ride singing through the shoreless air; — oft time
   Following the serpent lightning's winding track,
She ran upon the platforms of the wind,
And laughed to hear the fire-balls roar behind.

LVI.

And sometimes to those streams of upper air
   Which whirl the earth in its diurnal round,
She would ascend, and win the spirits there
   To let her join their chorus.   Mortals found
That on those days the sky was calm and fair,
   And mystic snatches of harmonious sound
Wandered upon the earth where'er she past,
And happy thoughts of hope, too sweet to last.

LVII.

But her choice sport was, in the hours of sleep,
   To glide adown old Nilus, where he threads
Egypt and Æthiopia, from the steep
   Of utmost Axumè, until he spreads,
Like a calm flock of silver-fleecèd sheep,
   His waters on the plain: and crested heads
Of cities and proud temples gleam amid,
And many a vapour-belted pyramid.

LVIII.

By Mœris and the Mareotid lakes,
   Strewn with faint blooms like bridal chamber floors,
Where naked boys bridling tame water-snakes,
   Or charioteering ghastly alligators,
Had left on the sweet waters mighty wakes
   Of those huge forms — within the brazen doors
Of the great Labyrinth slept both boy and beast,
Tired with the pomp of their Osirian feast.

LIX.

And where within the surface of the river
   The shadows of the massy temples lie,
And never are erased — but tremble ever
   Like things which every cloud can doom to die,
Through lotus-paven canals, and wheresoever
   The works of man pierced that serenest sky
With tombs, and towers, and fanes, 'twas her delight
To wander in the shadow of the night.

LX.

With motion like the spirit of that wind
   Whose soft step deepens slumber, her light feet
Past through the peopled haunts of human kind,
   Scattering sweet visions from her presence sweet,

Through fane, and palace-court, and labyrinth mined
   With many a dark and subterranean street
Under the Nile, through chambers high and deep
She past, observing mortals in their sleep.

LXI.

A pleasure sweet doubtless it was to see
   Mortals subdued in all the shapes of sleep.
Here lay two sister twins in infancy;
   There, a lone youth who in his dreams did weep;
Within, two lovers linkèd innocently
   In their loose locks which over both did creep
Like ivy from one stem;—and there lay calm
Old age with snow-bright hair and folded palm.

LXII.

But other troubled forms of sleep she saw,
   Not to be mirrored in a holy song —
Distortions foul of supernatural awe,
   And pale imaginings of visioned wrong;
And all the code of custom's lawless law
   Written upon the brows of old and young:
"This," said the wizard maiden, " is the strife
Which stirs the liquid surface of man's life."

LXIII.

And little did the sight disturb her soul. —
  We, the weak mariners of that wide lake
Where'er its shores extend or billows roll,
  Our course unpiloted and starless make
O'er its wild surface to an unknown goal: —
  But she in the calm depths her way could take,
Where in bright bowers immortal forms abide
Beneath the weltering of the restless tide.

LXIV.

And she saw princes couched under the glow
  Of sunlike gems; and round each temple-court
In dormitories ranged, row after row,
  She saw the priests asleep — all of one sort —
For all were educated to be so. —
  The peasants in their huts, and in the port
The sailors she saw cradled on the waves,
And the dead lulled within their dreamless graves.

LXV.

And all the forms in which those spirits lay
  Were to her sight like the diaphanous
Veils, in which those sweet ladies oft array
  Their delicate limbs, who would conceal from us

Only their scorn of all concealment: they
   Move in the light of their own beauty thus.
But these and all now lay with sleep upon them,
And little thought a Witch was looking on them.

LXVI.

She, all those human figures breathing there,
   Beheld as living spirits — to her eyes
The naked beauty of the soul lay bare,
   And often through a rude and worn disguise
She saw the inner form most bright and fair —
   And then she had a charm of strange device,
Which, murmured on mute lips with tender tone,
Could make that spirit mingle with her own.

LXVII.

Alas! Aurora, what wouldst thou have given
   For such a charm when Tithon became grey?
Or how much, Venus, of thy silver Heaven
   Wouldst thou have yielded, ere Proserpina
Had half (oh! why not all?) the debt forgiven
   Which dear Adonis had been doomed to pay,
To any witch who would have taught you it?
The Heliad doth not know its value yet.

LXVIII.

'Tis said in after times her spirit free
  Knew what love was, and felt itself alone —
But holy Dian could not chaster be
  Before she stooped to kiss Endymion,
Than now this lady — like a sexless bee
  Tasting all blossoms, and confined to none,
Among those mortal forms, the wizard-maiden
Past with an eye serene and heart unladen.

LXIX.

To those she saw most beautiful, she gave
  Strange panacea in a crystal bowl : —
They drank in their deep sleep of that sweet wave,
  And lived thenceforward as if some controul,
Mightier than life, were in them ; and the grave
  Of such, when death oppressed the weary soul,
Was as a green and overarching bower
Lit by the gems of many a starry flower.

LXX.

For on the night when they were buried, she
  Restored the embalmers' ruining, and shook
The light out of the funeral lamps, to be
  A mimic day within that deathy nook ;

And she unwound the woven imagery
   Of second childhood's swaddling bands, and took
The coffin, its last cradle, from its niche,
And threw it with contempt into a ditch.

LXXI.

And there the body lay, age after age,
   Mute, breathing, beating, warm and undecaying,
Like one asleep in a green hermitage,
   With gentle smiles about its eyelids playing,
And living in its dreams beyond the rage
   Of death or life; while they were still arraying
In liveries ever new, the rapid, blind
And fleeting generations of mankind.

LXXII.

And she would write strange dreams upon the brain
   Of those who were less beautiful, and make
All harsh and crooked purposes more vain
   Than in the desart is the serpent's wake
Which the sand covers, — all his evil gain
   The miser in such dreams would rise and shake
Into a beggar's lap; — the lying scribe
Would his own lies betray without a bribe.

THE WITCH OF ATLAS.

LXXIII.

The priests would write an explanation full,
    Translating hieroglyphics into Greek,
How the god Apis really was a bull,
    And nothing more; and bid the herald stick
The same against the temple doors, and pull
    The old cant down; they licensed all to speak
Whate'er they thought of hawks, and cats, and geese,
By pastoral letters to each diocese.

LXXIV.

The king would dress an ape up in his crown
    And robes, and seat him on his glorious seat,
And on the right hand of the sunlike throne
    Would place a gaudy mock-bird to repeat
The chatterings of the monkey. — Every one
    Of the prone courtiers crawled to kiss the feet
Of their great Emperor, when the morning came,
And kissed — alas, how many kiss the same!

LXXV.

The soldiers dreamed that they were blacksmiths, and
    Walked out of quarters in somnambulism;
Round the red anvils you might see them stand
    Like Cyclopses in Vulcan's sooty abysm,

Beating their swords to ploughshares ; — in a band
  The gaolers sent those of the liberal schism
Free through the streets of Memphis, much, I wis
To the annoyance of king Amasis.

LXXVI.

And timid lovers who had been so coy,
  They hardly knew whether they loved or not,
Would rise out of their rest, and take sweet joy,
  To the fulfilment of their inmost thought ;
And when next day the maiden and the boy
  Met one another, both, like sinners caught,
Blushed at the thing which each believed was done
Only in fancy — till the tenth moon shone ;

LXXVII.

And then the Witch would let them take no ill :
  Of many thousand schemes which lovers find,
The Witch found one, — and so they took their fill
  Of happiness in marriage warm and kind.
Friends who, by practice of some envious skill,
  Were torn apart, a wide wound, mind from mind !
She did unite again with visions clear
Of deep affection and of truth sincere.

TO THE MOON.

LXXVIII.

These were the pranks she played among the cities
  Of mortal men, and what she did to sprites
And Gods, entangling them in her sweet ditties
  To do her will, and show their subtle slights,
I will declare another time; for it is
  A tale more fit for the weird winter nights,
Than for these garish summer days, when we
Scarcely believe much more than we can see.

THE WANING MOON.

And like a dying lady, lean and pale,
Who totters forth, wrapt in a gauzy veil,
Out of her chamber, led by the insane
And feeble wanderings of her fading brain,
The moon arose up in the murky east,
A white and shapeless mass.

TO THE MOON.

Art thou pale for weariness
Of climbing heaven and gazing on the earth,
  Wandering companionless
Among the stars that have a different birth,—
And ever changing, like a joyless eye
That finds no object worth its constancy?

LOVE'S PHILOSOPHY.

I.

The fountains mingle with the river,
   And the rivers with the ocean;
The winds of heaven mix for ever
   With a sweet emotion;
Nothing in the world is single;
   All things by a law divine
In one another's being mingle;—
   Why not I with thine?

II.

See the mountains kiss high heaven,
   And the waves clasp one another;
No sister flower would be forgiven,
   If it disdained it's brother;
And the sunlight clasps the earth,
   And the moonbeams kiss the sea:
What are all these kissings worth,
   If thou kiss not me?

ARETHUSA.

I.

Arethusa arose
From her couch of snows
In the Acroceraunian mountains, —
From cloud and from crag,
With many a jag,
Shepherding her bright fountains.
She leapt down the rocks,
With her rainbow locks
Streaming among the streams; —
Her steps paved with green
The downward ravine
Which slopes to the western gleams:
And gliding and springing
She went, ever singing,
In murmurs as soft as sleep;
The Earth seemed to love her,
And Heaven smiled above her,
As she lingered towards the deep.

II.

Then Alpheus bold,
On his glacier cold,
With his trident the mountains strook;
    And opened a chasm
    In the rocks;—with the spasm
All Erymanthus shook.
    And the black south wind
    It concealed behind
The urns of the silent snow,
    And earthquake and thunder
    Did rend in sunder
The bars of the springs below:
    The beard and the hair
    Of the River-god were
Seen through the torrent's sweep,
    As he followed the light
    Of the fleet nymph's flight
To the brink of the Dorian deep.

III.

"Oh, save me! Oh, guide me!
And bid the deep hide me,
For he grasps me now by the hair!"
    The loud Ocean heard,
    To its blue depth stirred,
And divided at her prayer;

And under the water
The Earth's white daughter
Fled like a sunny beam;
Behind her descended
Her billows, unblended
With the brackish Dorian stream:—
Like a gloomy stain
On the emerald main
Alpheus rushed behind,—
As an eagle pursuing
A dove to its ruin
Down the streams of the cloudy wind.

IV.

Under the bowers
Where the Ocean Powers
Sit on their pearlèd thrones,
Through the coral woods
Of the weltering floods,
Over heaps of unvalued stones;
Through the dim beams
Which amid the streams
Weave a net-work of coloured light;
And under the caves,
Where the shadowy waves
Are as green as the forest's night:—

ARETHUSA.

    Outspeeding the shark,
    And the sword-fish dark,
Under the ocean foam,
    And up through the rifts
    Of the mountain clifts
They past to their Dorian home.

v.

    And now from their fountains
    In Enna's mountains,
Down one vale where the morning basks,
    Like friends once parted
    Grown single-hearted,
They ply their watery tasks.
    At sunrise they leap
    From their cradles steep
In the cave of the shelving hill;
    At noon-tide they flow
    Through the woods below
And the meadows of Asphodel;
    And at night they sleep
    In the rocking deep
Beneath the Ortygian shore; —
    Like spirits that lie
    In the azure sky
When they love but live no more.

THE QUESTION.

I.

I DREAMED that, as I wandered by the way,
  Bare winter suddenly was changed to spring,
And gentle odours led my steps astray,
  Mixed with a sound of waters murmuring
Along a shelving bank of turf, which lay
  Under a copse, and hardly dared to fling
Its green arms round the bosom of the stream,
But kissed it and then fled, as thou mightest in dream

II.

There grew pied wind-flowers and violets,
  Daisies, those pearled Arcturi of the earth,
The constellated flower that never sets;
  Faint oxlips; tender bluebells, at whose birth
The sod scarce heaved; and that tall flower that wets
  Like a child, half in tenderness and mirth —
Its mother's face with heaven-collected tears,
When the low wind, its playmate's voice, it hears.

III.

And in the warm hedge grew lush eglantine,
   Green cow-bind and the moonlight-coloured May,
And cherry blossoms, and white cups, whose wine
   Was the bright dew yet drained not by the day;
And wild roses, and ivy serpentine,
   With its dark buds and leaves, wandering astray;
And flowers azure, black, and streaked with gold,
Fairer than any wakened eyes behold.

IV.

And nearer to the river's trembling edge
   There grew broad flag-flowers, purple prankt with white,
And starry river buds among the sedge,
   And floating water-lilies, broad and bright,
Which lit the oak that overhung the hedge
   With moonlight beams of their own watery light;
And bulrushes, and reeds of such deep green
As soothed the dazzled eye with sober sheen.

V.

Methought that of these visionary flowers
   I made a nosegay, bound in such a way
That the same hues, which in their natural bowers
   Were mingled or opposed, the like array

Kept these imprisoned children of the Hours
　Within my hand, — and then, elate and gay,
I hastened to the spot whence I had come,
That I might there present it ! — Oh ! to whom ?

GOOD NIGHT.

I.

Good night? ah ! no ; the hour is ill
　Which severs those it should unite ;
Let us remain together still,
　Then it will be *good* night.

II.

How can I call the lone night good,
　Though thy sweet wishes wing its flight?
Be it not said, thought, understood,
　Then it will be *good* night.

III.

To hearts which near each other move
　From evening close to morning light,
The night is good ; because, my love,
　They never *say* good night.

HYMN OF APOLLO.

I.

The sleepless Hours who watch me as I lie,
  Curtained with star-inwoven tapestries,
From the broad moonlight of the sky,
  Fanning the busy dreams from my dim eyes,—
Waken me when their Mother, the grey Dawn,
Tells them that dreams and that the moon is gone.

II.

Then I arise, and climbing Heaven's blue dome,
  I walk over the mountains and the waves,
Leaving my robe upon the ocean foam;
  My footsteps pave the clouds with fire; the caves
Are filled with my bright presence, and the air
Leaves the green earth to my embraces bare.

III.

The sunbeams are my shafts, with which I kill
  Deceit, that loves the night and fears the day;
All men who do or even imagine ill
  Fly me, and from the glory of my ray
Good minds and open actions take new might,
Until diminished by the reign of night.

IV.

I feed the clouds, the rainbows and the flowers
  With their ætherial colours; the Moon's globe
And the pure stars in their eternal bowers
  Are cinctured with my power as with a robe;
Whatever lamps on Earth or Heaven may shine,
Are portions of one power, which is mine.

V.

I stand at noon upon the peak of Heaven,
  Then with unwilling steps I wander down
Into the clouds of the Atlantic even;
  For grief that I depart they weep and frown:
What look is more delightful than the smile
With which I soothe them from the western isle?

VI.

I am the eye with which the Universe
  Beholds itself and knows itself divine;
All harmony of instrument or verse,
  All prophecy, all medicine are mine,
All light of art or nature;—to my song,
Victory and praise in their own right belong.

HYMN OF PAN.

I.

From the forests and highlands
    We come, we come;
From the river-girt islands,
    Where loud waves are dumb
        Listening to my sweet pipings.
The wind in the reeds and the rushes,
    The bees on the bells of thyme,
The birds on the myrtle bushes,
    The cicale above in the lime,
And the lizards below in the grass,
Were as silent as ever old Tmolus was,
        Listening to my sweet pipings.

II.

Liquid Peneus was flowing,
    And all dark Tempe lay
In Pelion's shadow, outgrowing
    The light of the dying day,
        Speeded by my sweet pipings.
The Sileni, and Sylvans, and Fauns,
    And the Nymphs of the woods and waves,

HYMN OF PAN.

To the edge of the moist river-lawns,
   And the brink of the dewy caves,
And all that did then attend and follow
Were silent with love, as you now, Apollo,
      With envy of my sweet pipings.

III.

I sang of the dancing stars,
   I sang of the dædal Earth,
And of Heaven — and the giant wars,
   And Love, and Death, and Birth, —
      And then I changed my pipings, —
Singing how down the vale of Menalus
   I pursued a maiden and clasped a reed:
Gods and men, we are all deluded thus!
   It breaks in our bosom and then we bleed:
All wept, as I think both ye now would,
If envy or age had not frozen your blood,
      At the sorrow of my sweet pipings.

THE TWO SPIRITS.

AN ALLEGORY.

First Spirit.

O thou, who plumed with strong desire
   Wouldst float above the earth, beware !
A Shadow tracks thy flight of fire —
      Night is coming !
   Bright are the regions of the air,
And among the winds and beams
   It were delight to wander there —
      Night is coming !

Second Spirit.

The deathless stars are bright above ;
   If I would cross the shade of night,
Within my heart is the lamp of love,
      And that is day !
   And the moon will smile with gentle light
On my golden plumes where'er they move ;
   The meteors will linger round my flight,
      And make night day.

THE TWO SPIRITS.

First Spirit.

But if the whirlwinds of darkness waken
   Hail, and lightning, and stormy rain;
See, the bounds of the air are shaken —
     Night is coming!
The red swift clouds of the hurricane
Yon declining sun have overtaken,
   The clash of the hail sweeps over the plain —
     Night is coming!

Second Spirit.

I see the light, and I hear the sound;
   I 'll sail on the flood of the tempest dark,
With the calm within and the light around
     Which makes night day:
And thou, when the gloom is deep and stark,
Look from thy dull earth, slumber-bound,
   My moon-like flight thou then may'st mark
     On high, far away.

   Some say there is a precipice
     Where one vast pine is frozen to ruin
O'er piles of snow and chasms of ice
     'Mid Alpine mountains;

And that the languid storm pursuing
That wingèd shape, for ever flies
  Round those hoar branches, aye renewing
    Its aëry fountains.

Some say when nights are dry and clear,
  And the death-dews sleep on the morass,
Sweet whispers are heard by the traveller,
    Which make night day:
And a silver shape like his early love doth pass
Upborne by her wild and glittering hair,
  And when he awakes on the fragrant grass,
    He finds night day.

TO ———.

I.

I FEAR thy kisses, gentle maiden,
  Thou needest not fear mine;
My spirit is too deeply laden
  Ever to burthen thine.

II.

I fear thy mien, thy tones, thy motion,
  Thou needest not fear mine;
Innocent is the heart's devotion
  With which I worship thine.

SONG OF PROSERPINE,

WHILE GATHERING FLOWERS ON THE PLAIN OF ENNA.

I.

Sacred Goddess, Mother Earth,
   Thou from whose immortal bosom,
Gods, and men, and beasts have birth,
   Leaf and blade, and bud and blossom,
Breathe thine influence most divine
On thine own child, Proserpine.

II.

If with mists of evening dew
   Thou dost nourish these young flowers
Till they grow, in scent and hue,
   Fairest children of the hours,
Breathe thine influence most divine
On thine own child, Proserpine.

SUMMER AND WINTER.

It was a bright and cheerful afternoon,
Towards the end of the sunny month of June,
When the north wind congregates in crowds
The floating mountains of the silver clouds
From the horizon — and the stainless sky
Opens beyond them like eternity.
All things rejoiced beneath the sun; the weeds,
The river, and the corn-fields, and the reeds;
The willow leaves that glanced in the light breeze,
And the firm foliage of the larger trees.

It was a winter such as when birds die
In the deep forests; and the fishes lie
Stiffened in the translucent ice, which makes
Even the mud and slime of the warm lakes
A wrinkled clod as hard as brick; and when,
Among their children, comfortable men
Gather about great fires, and yet feel cold:
Alas then for the homeless beggar old!

ODE TO NAPLES.

EPODE I. α.

I STOOD within the city disinterred;
    And heard the autumnal leaves like light footfalls
Of spirits passing through the streets; and heard
    The Mountain's slumberous voice at intervals
        Thrill through those roofless halls;
The oracular thunder penetrating shook
    The listening soul in my suspended blood;
I felt that Earth out of her deep heart spoke —
    I felt, but heard not: — through white columns glowed
        The isle-sustaining Ocean-flood,
A plane of light between two Heavens of azure:
    Around me gleamed many a bright sepulchre
Of whose pure beauty, Time, as if his pleasure
Were to spare Death, had never made erasure;
    But every living lineament was clear
    As in the sculptor's thought; and there
The wreaths of stony myrtle, ivy and pine,
    Like winter leaves o'ergrown by moulded snow,
    Seemed only not to move and grow
Because the crystal silence of the air
    Weighed on their life; even as the Power divine
    Which then lulled all things, brooded upon mine.

ODE TO NAPLES.

EPODE II. α.

  Then gentle winds arose
  With many a mingled close
Of wild Æolian sound and mountain-odour keen;
  And where the Baian ocean
  Welters with airlike motion,
Within, above, around its bowers of starry green,
 Moving the sea-flowers in those purple caves
  Even as the ever stormless atmosphere
   Floats o'er the Elysian realm,
 It bore me like an Angel, o'er the waves
  Of sunlight, whose swift pinnace of dewy air
   No storm can overwhelm;
   I sailed, where ever flows
   Under the calm Serene
   A spirit of deep emotion
   From the unknown graves
   Of the dead kings of Melody.
Shadowy Aornos darkened o'er the helm
The horizontal æther; heaven stript bare
Its depths over Elysium, where the prow
Made the invisible water white as snow;
From that Typhæan mount, Inarime
 There streamed a sunlight vapour, like the standard
   Of some ætherial host;
   Whilst from all the coast,

Louder and louder, gathering round, there wandered
Over the oracular woods and divine sea
Prophesyings which grew articulate —
They seize me — I must speak them — be they fate !

STROPHE α. 1.

Naples ! thou Heart of men which ever pantest
   Naked, beneath the lidless eye of heaven !
Elysian City which to calm inchantest
   The mutinous air and sea : they round theé, even
   As sleep round Love, are driven !
Metropolis of a ruined Paradise
   Long lost, late won, and yet but half regained !
Bright Altar of the bloodless sacrifice,
   Which armèd Victory offers up unstained
   To Love, the flower-enchained !
Thou which wert once, and then didst cease to be,
Now art, and henceforth ever shalt be, free,
   If Hope, and Truth, and Justice can avail,
       Hail, hail, all hail !

STROPHE β. 2.

    Thou youngest giant birth
    Which from the groaning earth
Leap'st, clothed in armour of impenetrable scale !
    Last of the Intercessors !
    Who 'gainst the Crowned Transgressors

Pleadest before God's love! Arrayed in Wisdom's mail,
    Wave thy lightning lance in mirth
    Nor let thy high heart fail,
Though from their hundred gates the leagued Oppressors,
    With hurried legions move!
    Hail, hail, all hail!

ANTISTROPHE α.

What though Cimmerian Anarchs dare blaspheme
    Freedom and thee? thy shield is as a mirror
To make their blind slaves see, and with fierce gleam
    To turn his hungry sword upon the wearer;
        A new Actæon's error
Shall their's have been — devoured by their own hounds!
    Be thou like the imperial Basilisk
Killing thy foe with unapparent wounds!
    Gaze on oppression, till at that dread risk
    Aghast she pass from the Earth's disk:
Fear not, but gaze — for freemen mightier grow,
And slaves more feeble, gazing on their foe;
    If Hope and Truth and Justice may avail,
    Thou shalt be great — All hail!

ANTISTROPHE β. 2.

    From Freedom's form divine,
    From Nature's inmost shrine,

Strip every impious gawd, rend Error veil by veil:
    O'er Ruin desolate,
    O'er Falsehood's fallen state,
Sit thou sublime, unawed; be the Destroyer pale!
    And equal laws be thine,
    And wingèd words let sail,
Freighted with truth even from the throne of God:
    That wealth, surviving fate,
    Be thine. — All hail!

ANTISTROPHE α. γ.

Didst thou not start to hear Spain's thrilling pæan
  From land to land re-echoed solemnly,
Till silence became music? From the Ææan
    To the cold Alps, eternal Italy
    Starts to hear thine! The Sea
Which paves the desert streets of Venice laughs
  In light and music; widowed Genoa wan
By moonlight spells ancestral epitaphs,
  Murmuring, where is Doria? fair Milan,
    Within whose veins long ran
The viper's palsying venom, lifts her heel
To bruise his head. The signal and the seal
  (If Hope and Truth and Justice can avail)
  Art Thou of all these hopes. — O hail!

ODE TO NAPLES.

ANTISTROPHE β. γ.

Florence! beneath the sun,
Of cities fairest one,
Blushes within her bower for Freedom's expectation:
From eyes of quenchless hope
Rome tears the priestly cope,
As ruling once by power, so now by admiration,
As athlete stript to run
From a remoter station
For the high prize lost on Philippi's shore:—
As then Hope, Truth, and Justice did avail,
So now may Fraud and Wrong! O hail!

EPODE I. β.

Hear ye the march as of the Earth-born Forms
Arrayed against the ever-living Gods?
The crash and darkness of a thousand storms
Bursting their inaccessible abodes
Of crags and thunder-clouds?
See ye the banners blazoned to the day,
Inwrought with emblems of barbaric pride?
Dissonant threats kill Silence far away,
The serene Heaven which wraps our Eden wide
With iron light is dyed,
The Anarchs of the North lead forth their legions

Like Chaos o'er creation, uncreating;
An hundred tribes nourished on strange religions
And lawless slaveries,—down the aërial regions
  Of the white Alps, desolating,
 Famished wolves that bide no waiting,
Blotting the glowing footsteps of old glory,
Trampling our columned cities into dust,
  Their dull and savage lust
 On Beauty's corse to sickness satiating,—
They come! The fields they tread look black and hoary
With fire—from their red feet the streams run gory!

EPODE II. β.

 Great Spirit, deepest Love!
 Which rulest and dost move
All things which live and are, within the Italian shore;
  Who spreadest heaven around it,
  Whose woods, rocks, waves, surround it;
Who sittest in thy star, o'er Ocean's western floor,
Spirit of beauty! at whose soft command
 The sunbeams and the showers distil its foison
  From the Earth's bosom chill;
O bid those beams be each a blinding brand
 Of lightning! bid those showers be dews of poison!
  Bid the Earth's plenty kill!
  Bid thy bright Heaven above,

    Whilst light and darkness bound it,
    Be their tomb who planned
    To make it ours and thine!
Or, with thine harmonizing ardours fill
And raise thy sons, as o'er the prone horizon
Thy lamp feeds every twilight wave with fire—
Be man's high hope and unextinct desire,
The instrument to work thy will divine!
    Then clouds from sunbeams, antelopes from leopards,
        And frowns and fears from Thee,
        Would not more swiftly flee
    Than Celtic wolves from the Ausonian shepherds.—
Whatever, Spirit, from thy starry shrine
  Thou yieldest or withholdest, Oh let be
  This city of thy worship ever free!

LIBERTY.

I.

The fiery mountains answer each other;
  Their thunderings are echoed from zone to zone;
The tempestuous oceans awake one another,
    And the ice-rocks are shaken round Winter's throne,
      When the clarion of the Typhoon is blown.

LIBERTY.

II.

From a single cloud the lightning flashes,
   Whilst a thousand isles are illumined around,
Earthquake is trampling one city to ashes,
   An hundred are shuddering and tottering; the sound
     Is bellowing underground.

III.

But keener thy gaze than the lightning's glare,
   And swifter thy step than the earthquake's tramp;
Thou deafenest the rage of the ocean; thy stare
   Makes blind the volcanoes; the sun's bright lamp
     To thine is a fen-fire damp.

IV.

From billow and mountain and exhalation
   The sunlight is darted through vapour and blast;
From spirit to spirit, from nation to nation,
   From city to hamlet thy dawning is cast, —
And tyrants and slaves are like shadows of night
     In the van of the morning light.

THE WORLD'S WANDERERS.

I.

Tell me, thou star, whose wings of light
Speed thee in thy fiery flight,
In what cavern of the night
    Will thy pinions close now?

II.

Tell me, moon, thou pale and grey
Pilgrim of heaven's homeless way,
In what depth of night or day
    Seekest thou repose now?

III.

Weary wind, who wanderest
Like the world's rejected guest,
Hast thou still some secret nest
    On the tree or billow?

AN ALLEGORY.

I.

A PORTAL as of shadowy adamant
   Stands yawning on the highway of the life
Which we all tread, a cavern huge and gaunt;
   Around it rages an unceasing strife
Of shadows, like the restless clouds that haunt
The gap of some cleft mountain, lifted high
Into the whirlwinds of the upper sky.

II.

And many pass it by with careless tread,
   Not knowing that a shadowy . . .
Tracks every traveller even to where the dead
   Wait peacefully for their companion new;
But others, by more curious humour led,
   Pause to examine, — these are very few,
And they learn little there, except to know
That shadows follow them where'er they go.

TIME LONG PAST.

I.

Like the ghost of a dear friend dead
  Is time long past.
A tone which is now forever fled,
A hope which is now forever past,
A love so sweet it could not last,
  Was time long past.

II.

There were sweet dreams in the night
  Of time long past:
And, was it sadness or delight,
Each day a shadow onward cast
Which made us wish it yet might last—
  That time long past.

III.

There is regret, almost remorse,
  For time long past.

SONNET.

'Tis like a child's belovèd corse
A father watches, till at last
Beauty is like remembrance cast
  From time long past

SONNET.

Ye hasten to the dead! What seek ye there,
Ye restless thoughts and busy purposes
Of the idle brain, which the world's livery wear?
O thou quick Heart which pantest to possess
All that anticipation feigneth fair!
Thou vainly curious mind which wouldest guess
Whence thou didst come, and whither thou mayst go,
And that which never yet was known wouldst know,—
Oh, whither hasten ye that thus ye press
With such swift feet life's green and pleasant path,
Seeking alike from happiness and woe
A refuge in the cavern of grey death?
O heart, and mind, and thoughts! What thing do you
Hope to inherit in the grave below?

LINES TO A REVIEWER.

Alas! good friend, what profit can you see
In hating such an hateless thing as me?
There is no sport in hate where all the rage
Is on one side. In vain would you assuage
Your frowns upon an unresisting smile,
In which not even contempt lurks, to beguile
Your heart, by some faint sympathy of hate.
Oh conquer what you cannot satiate!
For to your passion I am far more coy
Than ever yet was coldest maid or boy
In winter noon. Of your antipathy
If I am the Narcissus, you are free
To pine into a sound with hating me.

FRAGMENT ON KEATS,

WHO DESIRED THAT ON HIS TOMB SHOULD BE INSCRIBED—

"Here lieth One whose name was writ on water."
   But, ere the breath that could erase it blew,
Death, in remorse for that fell slaughter,
   Death, the immortalizing winter, flew   [grew
   Athwart the stream,—and time's printless torrent
A scroll of crystal, blazoning the name
   Of Adonais.——

ADONAIS.

I.

I weep for Adonais — he is dead!
O, weep for Adonais! though our tears
Thaw not the frost which binds so dear a head!
And thou, sad Hour, selected from all years'
To mourn our loss, rouse thy obscure compeers,
And teach them thine own sorrow, say: with me
Died Adonais; till the Future dares
Forget the Past, his fate and fame shall be
An echo and a light unto eternity!

II.

Where wert thou mighty Mother, when he lay,
When thy Son lay, pierced by the shaft which flies
In darkness? where was lorn Urania
When Adonais died? With veilèd eyes,
'Mid listening Echoes, in her Paradise
She sate, while one, with soft enamoured breath,
Rekindled all the fading melodies,
With which, like flowers that mock the corse beneath,
He had adorned and hid the coming bulk of death.

III.

O, weep for Adonais — he is dead!
Wake, melancholy Mother, wake and weep!
Yet wherefore? Quench within their burning bed
Thy fiery tears, and let thy loud heart keep
Like his, a mute and uncomplaining sleep;
For he is gone, where all things wise and fair
Descend;— oh, dream not that the amorous Deep
Will yet restore him to the vital air;
Death feeds on his mute voice, and laughs at our despair.

IV.

Most musical of mourners, weep again!
Lament anew, Urania!— He died,
Who was the Sire of an immortal strain,
Blind, old, and lonely, when his country's pride,
The priest, the slave, and the liberticide,
Trampled and mocked with many a loathèd rite
Of lust and blood; he went, unterrified,
Into the gulf of death; but his clear Sprite
Yet reigns o'er earth; the third among the sons of light.

V.

Most musical of mourners, weep anew!
Not all to that bright station dared to climb;

And happier they their happiness who knew,
Whose tapers yet burn through that night of time
In which suns perished; others more sublime,
Struck by the envious wrath of man or God,
Have sunk, extinct in their refulgent prime;
And some yet live, treading the thorny road,
Which leads, through toil and hate, to Fame's serene
  abode.

VI.

But now, thy youngest, dearest one has perished,
The nursling of thy widowhood, who grew,
Like a pale flower by some sad maiden cherished,
And fed with true love tears, instead of dew;
Most musical of mourners, weep anew!
Thy extreme hope, the loveliest and the last,
The bloom, whose petals nipt before they blew
Died on the promise of the fruit, is waste;
The broken lily lies — the storm is overpast.

VII.

To that high Capital, where kingly Death
Keeps his pale court in beauty and decay,
He came; and bought, with price of purest breath,
A grave among the eternal. — Come away!
Haste, while the vault of blue Italian day

Is yet his fitting charnel-roof! while still
He lies, as if in dewy sleep he lay;
Awake him not! surely he takes his fill
Of deep and liquid rest, forgetful of all ill.

VIII.

He will awake no more, oh, never more! —
Within the twilight chamber spreads apace,
The shadow of white Death, and at the door
Invisible Corruption waits to trace
His extreme way to her dim dwelling-place;
The eternal Hunger sits, but pity and awe
Soothe her pale rage, nor dares she to deface
So fair a prey, till darkness, and the law
Of change, shall o'er his sleep the mortal curtain draw.

IX.

O, weep for Adonais! — The quick Dreams,
The passion-wingèd Ministers of thought,
Who were his flocks, whom near the living streams
Of his young spirit he fed, and whom he taught
The love which was its music, wander not, —
Wander no more, from kindling brain to brain,
But droop there, whence they sprung; and mourn their lot
Round the cold heart, where, after their sweet pain,
They ne'er will gather strength, or find a home again.

X.

And one with trembling hands clasps his cold head,
And fans him with her moonlight wings, and cries:
" Our love, our hope, our sorrow, is not dead;
" See, on the silken fringe of his faint eyes,
" Like dew upon a sleeping flower, there lies
" A tear some Dream has loosened from his brain."
Lost Angel of a ruined Paradise !
She knew not 'twas her own; as with no stain
She faded, like a cloud which had outwept its rain.

XI.

One from a lucid urn of starry dew
Washed his light limbs as if embalming them;
Another clipt her profuse locks, and threw
The wreath upon him, like an anadem,
Which frozen tears instead of pearls begem;
Another in her wilful grief would break
Her bow and wingèd reeds, as if to stem
A greater loss with one which was more weak;
And dull the barbèd fire against his frozen cheek.

XII.

Another Splendour on his mouth alit,
That mouth, whence it was wont to draw the breath
Which gave it strength to pierce the guarded wit,
And pass into the panting heart beneath

ADONAIS.

With lightning and with music: the damp death
Quenched its caress upon his icy lips;
And, as a dying meteor stains a wreath
Of moonlight vapour, which the cold night clips,
flushed through his pale limbs, and past to its eclipse.

XIII.

And others came ... Desires and Adorations,
Wingèd Persuasions and veiled Destinies,
Splendours, and Glooms, and glimmering Incarnations
Of hopes and fears, and twilight Phantasies;
And Sorrow, with her family of Sighs,
And Pleasure, blind with tears, led by the gleam
Of her own dying smile instead of eyes,
Came in slow pomp; — the moving pomp might seem
ke pageantry of mist on an autumnal stream.

XIV.

All he had loved, and moulded into thought,
From shape, and hue, and odour, and sweet sound,
Lamented Adonais. Morning sought
Her eastern watchtower, and her hair unbound,
Wet with the tears which should adorn the ground,
Dimmed the aerial eyes that kindle day;
Afar the melancholy thunder moaned,
Pale Ocean in unquiet slumber lay,
ad the wild winds flew round, sobbing in their dismay.

XV.

Lost Echo sits amid the voiceless mountains,
And feeds her grief with his remembered lay,
And will no more reply to winds or fountains,
Or amorous birds perched on the young green spray,
Or herdsman's horn, or bell at closing day;
Since she can mimic not his lips, more dear
Than those for whose disdain she pined away
Into a shadow of all sounds: — a drear
Murmur, between their songs, is all the woodmen hear.

XVI.

Grief made the young Spring wild, and she threw down
Her kindling buds, as if she Autumn were,
Or they dead leaves; since her delight is flown
For whom should she have waked the sullen year?
To Phœbus was not Hyacinth so dear
Nor to himself Narcissus, as to both
Thou Adonais: wan they stand and sere
Amid the faint companions of their youth,
With dew all turned to tears; odour, to sighing ruth.

XVII.

Thy spirit's sister, the lorn nightingale
Mourns not her mate with such melodious pain;

ADONAIS.

Not so the eagle, who like thee could scale
Heaven, and could nourish in the sun's domain
Her mighty youth with morning, doth complain,
Soaring and screaming round her empty nest,
As Albion wails for thee: the curse of Cain
Light on his head who pierced thy innocent breast,
And scared the angel soul that was its earthly guest!

XVIII.

Ah woe is me! Winter is come and gone,
But grief returns with the revolving year;
The airs and streams renew their joyous tone;
The ants, the bees, the swallows reappear;
Fresh leaves and flowers deck the dead Seasons' bier;
The amorous birds now pair in every brake,
And build their mossy homes in field and brere;
And the green lizard, and the golden snake,
Like unimprisoned flames, out of their trance awake.

XIX.

Through wood and stream and field and hill and
    Ocean
A quickening life from the Earth's heart has burst
As it has ever done, with change and motion,
From the great morning of the world when first
God dawned on Chaos; in its steam immersed

The lamps of Heaven flash with a softer light;
All baser things pant with life's sacred thirst;
Diffuse themselves; and spend in love's delight,
The beauty and the joy of their renewèd might.

XX.

The leprous corpse touched by this spirit tender
Exhales itself in flowers of gentle breath;
Like incarnations of the stars, when splendour
Is changed to fragrance, they illumine death
And mock the merry worm that wakes beneath;
Nought we know, dies. Shall that alone which knows
Be as a sword consumed before the sheath
By sightless lightning? — th' intense atom glows
A moment, then is quenched in a most cold repose.

XXI.

Alas! that all we loved of him should be,
But for our grief, as if it had not been,
And grief itself be mortal! Woe is me!
Whence are we, and why are we? of what scene
The actors or spectators? Great and mean
Meet massed in death, who lends what life must
    borrow.
As long as skies are blue, and fields are green,
Evening must usher night, night urge the morrow,
Month follow month with woe, and year wake year to
    sorrow.

XXII.

He will awake no more, oh, never more!
"Wake thou," cried Misery, "childless Mother, rise
"Out of thy sleep, and slake, in thy heart's core,
"A wound more fierce than his with tears and sighs."
And all the Dreams that watched Urania's eyes,
And all the Echoes whom their sister's song
Had held in holy silence, cried: "Arise!"
Swift as a Thought by the snake Memory stung,
From her ambrosial rest the fading Splendour sprung.

XXIII.

She rose like an autumnal Night, that springs
Out of the East, and follows wild and drear
The golden Day, which, on eternal wings,
Even as a ghost abandoning a bier,
Had left the Earth a corpse. Sorrow and fear
So struck, so roused, so rapt Urania;
So saddened round her like an atmosphere
Of stormy mist; so swept her on her way
Even to the mournful place where Adonais lay.

XXIV.

Out of her secret Paradise she sped,
Through camps and cities rough with stone, and steel,

And human hearts, which to her aery tread
Yielding not, wounded the invisible
Palms of her tender feet where'er they fell:
And barbèd tongues, and thoughts more sharp than they
Rent the soft Form they never could repel,
Whose sacred blood, like the young tears of May,
Paved with eternal flowers that undeserving way.

XXV.

In the death chamber for a moment Death
Shamed by the presence of that living Might
Blushed to annihilation, and the breath
Revisited those lips, and life's pale light
Flashed through those limbs, so late her dear delight.
"Leave me not wild and drear and comfortless,
"As silent lightning leaves the starless night!
"Leave me not!" cried Urania: her distress
Roused Death: Death rose and smiled, and met her vain caress.

XXVI.

"Stay yet awhile! speak to me once again;
"Kiss me, so long but as a kiss may live;
"And in my heartless breast and burning brain
"That word, that kiss shall all thoughts else survive,

"With food of saddest memory kept alive,
"Now thou art dead, as if it were a part
"Of thee, my Adonais! I would give
"All that I am to be as thou now art!
"But I am chained to Time, and cannot thence depart!

XXVII.

"Oh gentle child, beautiful as thou wert,
"Why didst thou leave the trodden paths of men
"Too soon, and with weak hands though mighty heart
"Dare the unpastured dragon in his den?
"Defenceless as thou wert, oh where was then
"Wisdom the mirrored shield, or scorn the spear?
"Or hadst thou waited the full cycle, when
"Thy spirit should have filled its crescent sphere,
"The monsters of life's waste had fled from thee like deer.

XXVIII.

"The herded wolves, bold only to pursue;
"The obscene ravens, clamorous o'er the dead;
"The vultures to the conqueror's banner true
"Who feed where Desolation first has fed,
"And whose wings rain contagion; — how they fled,

"When like Apollo, from his golden bow,
"The Pythian of the age one arrow sped
"And smiled!—The spoilers tempt no second blow,
"They fawn on the proud feet that spurn them lying
  low.

XXIX.

"The sun comes forth, and many reptiles spawn;
"He sets, and each ephemeral insect then
"Is gathered into death without a dawn,
"And the immortal stars awake again;
"So is it in the world of living men:
"A godlike mind soars forth, in its delight
"Making earth bare and veiling heaven, and when
"It sinks, the swarms that dimmed or shared its
  light
"Leave to its kindred lamps the spirit's awful night."

XXX.

Thus ceased she: and the mountain shepherds came,
Their garlands sere, their magic mantles rent;
The Pilgrim of Eternity, whose fame
Over his living head like Heaven is bent,
An early but enduring monument,
Came, veiling all the lightnings of his song
In sorrow; from her wilds Ierne sent
The sweetest lyrist of her saddest wrong,
And love taught grief to fall like music from his tongue.

XXXI.

Midst others of less note, came one frail Form,
A phantom among men; companionless
As the last cloud of an expiring storm
Whose thunder is its knell; he, as I guess,
Had gazed on Nature's naked loveliness,
Actæon-like, and now he fled astray
With feeble steps o'er the world's wilderness,
And his own thoughts, along that rugged way,
Pursued, like raging hounds, their father and their prey.

XXXII.

A pardlike Spirit beautiful and swift —
A Love in desolation masked; — a Power
Girt round with weakness; — it can scarce uplift
The weight of the superincumbent hour;
It is a dying lamp, a falling shower,
A breaking billow; — even whilst we speak
Is it not broken? On the withering flower
The killing sun smiles brightly: on a cheek
The life can burn in blood, even while the heart may
      break.

XXXIII.

His head was bound with pansies overblown,
And faded violets, white, and pied, and blue;

And a light spear topped with a cypress cone,
Round whose rude shaft dark ivy tresses grew
Yet dripping with the forest's noonday dew,
Vibrated, as the ever-beating heart
Shook the weak hand that grasped it; of that crew
He came the last, neglected and apart;
A herd-abandoned deer struck by the hunter's dart.

XXXIV.

All stood aloof, and at his partial moan
Smiled through their tears; well knew that gentle band
Who in another's fate now wept his own;
As in the accents of an unknown land,
He sung new sorrow; sad Urania scanned
The Stranger's mien, and murmured: "who art thou?"
He answered not, but with a sudden hand
Made bare his branded and ensanguined brow,
Which was like Cain's or Christ's — Oh! that it should be so!

XXXV.

What softer voice is hushed over the dead?
Athwart what brow is that dark mantle thrown?
What form leans sadly o'er the white death-bed,
In mockery of monumental stone,

ADONAIS.

The heavy heart heaving without a moan?
If it be He, who, gentlest of the wise,
Taught, soothed, loved, honoured the departed one;
Let me not vex, with inharmonious sighs
The silence of that heart's accepted sacrifice:

XXXVI.

Our Adonais has drunk poison — oh!
What deaf and viperous murderer could crown
Life's early cup with such a draught of woe?
The nameless worm would now itself disown:
It felt, yet could escape the magic tone
Whose prelude held all envy, hate, and wrong,
But what was howling in one breast alone,
Silent with expectation of the song,
Whose master's hand is cold, whose silver lyre unstrung.

XXXVII.

Live thou, whose infamy is not thy fame!
Live! fear no heavier chastisement from me,
Thou noteless blot on a remembered name!
But be thyself, and know thyself to be!
And ever at thy season be thou free
To spill the venom when thy fangs o'erflow:
Remorse and Self-contempt shall cling to thee;
Hot Shame shall burn upon thy secret brow,
And like a beaten hound tremble thou shalt — as now.

XXXVIII.

Nor let us weep that our delight is fled
Far from these carrion kites that scream below;
He wakes or sleeps with the enduring dead;
Thou canst not soar where he is sitting now. —
Dust to the dust! but the pure spirit shall flow
Back to the burning fountain whence it came,
A portion of the Eternal, which must glow
Through time and change, unquenchably the same,
Whilst thy cold embers choke the sordid hearth of shame.

XXXIX.

Peace, peace! he is not dead, he doth not sleep —
He hath awakened from the dream of life —
'Tis we, who lost in stormy visions, keep
With phantoms an unprofitable strife,
And in mad trance, strike with our spirit's knife
Invulnerable nothings. — *We* decay
Like corpses in a charnel; fear and grief
Convulse us and consume us day by day,
And cold hopes swarm like worms within our living clay.

XL.

He has outsoared the shadow of our night;
Envy and calumny and hate and pain,

And that unrest which men miscall delight,
Can touch him not and torture not again;
From the contagion of the world's slow stain
He is secure, and now can never mourn
A heart grown cold, a head grown grey in vain;
Nor, when the spirit's self has ceased to burn,
With sparkless ashes load an unlamented urn. -

XLI.

He lives, he wakes — 'tis Death is dead, not he;
Mourn not for Adonais. — Thou young Dawn
Turn all thy dew to splendour, for from thee
The spirit thou lamentest is not gone;
Ye caverns and ye forests, cease to moan!
Cease ye faint flowers and fountains, and thou Air
Which like a mourning veil thy scarf hadst thrown
O'er the abandoned Earth, now leave it bare
Even to the joyous stars which smile on it's despair!

XLII.

He is made one with Nature: there is heard
His voice in all her music, from the moan
Of thunder, to the song of night's sweet bird;
He is a presence to be felt and known
In darkness and in light, from herb and stone,

ADONAIS.

Spreading itself where'er that Power may move
Which has withdrawn his being to its own;
Which wields the world with never wearied love,
Sustains it from beneath, and kindles it above.

XLIII.

He is a portion of the loveliness
Which once he made more lovely: he doth bear
His part, while the one Spirit's plastic stress
Sweeps through the dull dense world, compelling there
All new successions to the forms they wear;
Torturing th' unwilling dross that checks it's flight
To it's own likeness, as each mass may bear;
And bursting in it's beauty and it's might
From trees and beasts and men into the Heaven's light

XLIV.

The splendours of the firmament of time
May be eclipsed, but are extinguished not;
Like stars to their appointed height they climb
And death is a low mist which cannot blot
The brightness it may veil. When lofty thought
Lifts a young heart above its mortal lair,
And love and life contend in it, for what
Shall be its earthly doom, the dead live there
And move like winds of light on dark and stormy air.

XLV.

The inheritors of unfulfilled renown
Rose from their thrones, built beyond mortal thought,
Far in the Unapparent.   Chatterton
Rose pale, his solemn agony had not
Yet faded from him ; Sidney, as he fought
And as he fell and as he lived and loved
Sublimely mild, a Spirit without spot,
Arose ; and Lucan, by his death approved :
Oblivion as they rose shrank like a thing reproved.

XLVI.

And many more, whose names on Earth are dark
But whose transmitted effluence cannot die
So long as fire outlives the parent spark,
Rose, robed in dazzling immortality.
" Thou art become as one of us," they cry,
" It was for thee yon kingless sphere has long
" Swung blind in unascended majesty,
" Silent alone amid an Heaven of Song.
" Assume thy wingèd throne, thou Vesper of our throng ! "

XLVII.

Who mourns for Adonais ? oh come forth
Fond wretch ! and know thyself and him aright.
Clasp with thy panting soul the pendulous Earth ;
As from a centre, dart thy spirit's light

Beyond all worlds, until its spacious might
Satiate the void circumference : then shrink
Even to a point within our day and night;
And keep thy heart light lest it make thee sink
When hope has kindled hope, and lured thee to the brink.

XLVIII.

Or go to Rome, which is the sepulchre
O, not of him, but of our joy : 'tis nought
That ages, empires, and religions there
Lie buried in the ravage they have wrought;
For such as he can lend, — they borrow not
Glory from those who made the world their prey;
And he is gathered to the kings of thought
Who waged contention with their time's decay,
And of the past are all that cannot pass away.

XLIX.

Go thou to Rome, — at once the Paradise,
The grave, the city, and the wilderness;
And where its wrecks like shattered mountains rise,
And flowering weeds, and fragrant copses dress
The bones of Desolation's nakedness
Pass, till the Spirit of the spot shall lead
Thy footsteps to a slope of green access
Where, like an infant's smile, over the dead,
A light of laughing flowers along the grass is spread.

L.

And gray walls moulder round, on which dull Time
Feeds, like slow fire upon a hoary brand;
And one keen pyramid with wedge sublime,
Pavilioning the dust of him who planned
This refuge for his memory, doth stand
Like flame transformed to marble; and beneath,
A field is spread, on which a newer band
Have pitched in Heaven's smile their camp of death
elcoming him we lose with scarce extinguished breath.

LI.

Here pause: these graves are all too young as yet
To have outgrown the sorrow which consigned
Its charge to each; and if the seal is set,
Here, on one fountain of a mourning mind,
Break it not thou! too surely shalt thou find
Thine own well full, if thou returnest home,
Of tears and gall. From the world's bitter wind
Seek shelter in the shadow of the tomb.
hat Adonais is, why fear we to become?

LII.

The One remains, the many change and pass;
Heaven's light forever shines, Earth's shadows fly;

Life, like a dome of many-coloured glass,
Stains the white radiance of Eternity,
Until Death tramples it to fragments. — Die,
If thou wouldst be with that which thou dost seek !
Follow where all is fled ! — Rome's azure sky,
Flowers, ruins, statues, music, words, are weak
The glory they transfuse with fitting truth to speak.

LIII.

Why linger, why turn back, why shrink, my Heart?
Thy hopes are gone before : from all things here
They have departed ; thou shouldst now depart !
A light is past from the revolving year,
And man, and woman ; and what still is dear
Attracts to crush, repels to make thee wither.
The soft sky smiles, — the low wind whispers near ;
'Tis Adonais calls ! oh, hasten thither,
No more let Life divide what Death can join together.

LIV.

That Light whose smile kindles the Universe,
That Beauty in which all things work and move,
That Benediction which the eclipsing Curse
Of birth can quench not, that sustaining Love
Which through the web of being blindly wove

By man and beast and earth and air and sea,
Burns bright or dim, as each are mirrors of
  The fire for which all thirst; now beams on me,
Consuming the last clouds of cold mortality.

LV.

The breath whose might I have invoked in song
Descends on me; my spirit's bark is driven,
  Far from the shore, far from the trembling throng
Whose sails were never to the tempest given;
The massy earth and spherèd skies are riven!
  I am borne darkly, fearfully, afar;
Whilst burning through the inmost veil of Heaven,
  The soul of Adonais, like a star,
Beacons from the abode where the Eternal are.

ON THE DEATH OF NAPOLEON.

WRITTEN ON HEARING THE NEWS OF THE DEATH OF NAPOLEON.

WHAT! alive and so bold, oh earth?
   Art thou not overbold?
   What! leapest thou forth as of old
In the light of thy morning mirth,
The last of the flock of the starry fold?
Ha! leapest thou forth as of old?
Are not the limbs still when the ghost is fled,
And canst thou move, Napoleon being dead?

How! is not thy quick heart cold?
   What spark is alive on thy hearth?
How! is not *his* death-knell knolled?
   And livest *thou* still, Mother Earth?
Thou wert warming thy fingers old
O'er the embers covered and cold
Of that most fiery spirit, when it fled—
What, Mother, do you laugh now he is dead?

"Who has known me of old," replied Earth,
   "Or who has my story told?
   It is thou who art overbold."

ON THE DEATH OF NAPOLEON.

And the lightning of scorn laughed forth
As she sung, " to my bosom I fold
All my sons when their knell is knolled,
And so with living motion all are fed,
And the quick spring like weeds out of the dead.

" Still alive and still bold," shouted Earth,
   " I grow bolder and still more bold.
   The dead fill me ten thousand fold
Fuller of speed, and splendour, and mirth,
I was cloudy, and sullen, and cold,
Like a frozen chaos uprolled,
Till by the spirit of the mighty dead
My heart grew warm. I feed on whom I fed.

" Aye, alive and still bold," muttered Earth,
   " Napoleon's fierce spirit rolled,
   In terror and blood and gold,
A torrent of ruin to death from his birth.
Leave the millions who follow to mould
The metal before it be cold;
And weave into his shame, which like the dead
Shrouds me, the hopes that from his glory fled."

DIRGE FOR THE YEAR.

I.

ORPHAN hours, the year is dead,
   Come and sigh, come and weep!
Merry hours, smile instead,
   For the year is but asleep.
See, it smiles as it is sleeping,
Mocking your untimely weeping.

II.

As an earthquake rocks a corse
   In its coffin in the clay,
So White Winter, that rough nurse,
   Rocks the death-cold year to-day;
Solemn hours! wail aloud
For your mother in her shroud.

III.

As the wild air stirs and sways
   The tree-swung cradle of a child,
So the breath of these rude days
   Rocks the year:— be calm and mild,
Trembling hours, she will arise
With new love within her eyes.

IV.

January grey is here,
    Like a sexton by her grave;
February bears the bier,
    March with grief doth howl and rave.
And April weeps — but, O, ye hours,
Follow with May's fairest flowers.

TO NIGHT.

I.

SWIFTLY walk over the western wave,
    Spirit of Night!
Out of the misty eastern cave,
Where all the long and lone daylight,
Thou wovest dreams of joy and fear,
Which make thee terrible and dear, —
    Swift be thy flight!

II.

Wrap thy form in a mantle grey,
    Star-inwrought!
Blind with thine hair the eyes of Day;
Kiss her until she be wearied out,
Then wander o'er city, and sea, and land,
Touching all with thine opiate wand —
    Come, long sought!

TO NIGHT.

III.

When I arose and saw the dawn,
   I sighed for thee;
When light rode high, and the dew was gone,
And noon lay heavy on flower and tree,
And the weary Day turned to his rest,
Lingering like an unloved guest,
   I sighed for thee.

IV.

Thy brother Death came, and cried,
   Wouldst thou me?
Thy sweet child Sleep, the filmy-eyed,
   Murmured like a noon-tide bee,
Shall I nestle near thy side?
Wouldst thou me? — And I replied,
   No, not thee!

V.

Death will come when thou art dead,
   Soon, too soon —
Sleep will come when thou art fled;
Of neither would I ask the boon
I ask of thee, belovèd Night —
Swift be thine approaching flight,
   Come soon, soon!

TO EMILIA VIVIANI.

MADONNA, wherefore hast thou sent to me
   Sweet basil and mignonette?
Embleming love and health, which never yet
In the same wreath might be.
   Alas, and they are wet!
Is it with thy kisses or thy tears?
     For never rain or dew
     Such fragrance drew
From plant or flower — the very doubt endears
    My sadness ever new,
The sighs I breathe, the tears I shed for thee.

TIME.

UNFATHOMABLE Sea! whose waves are years,
   Ocean of Time, whose waters of deep woe
Are brackish with the salt of human tears!
   Thou shoreless flood, which in thy ebb and flow
Claspest the limits of mortality!
And sick of prey, yet howling on for more,
Vomitest thy wrecks on its inhospitable shore;
   Treacherous in calm, and terrible in storm,
     Who shall put forth on thee,
     Unfathomable Sea?

CHORUS FROM HELLAS.

We strew these opiate flowers
    On thy restless pillow, —
They were stripped from Orient bowers,
    By the Indian billow.
        Be thy sleep
        Calm and deep,
Like their's who fell — not our's who weep !

Away, unlovely dreams !
    Away, false shapes of sleep !
Be his, as Heaven seems,
    Clear, and bright, and deep !
Soft as love, and calm as death,
Sweet as a summer night without a breath.

Sleep, sleep ! our song is laden
    With the soul of slumber;
It was sung by a Samian maiden,
    Whose lover was of the number
        Who now keep
        That calm sleep
Whence none may wake, where none shall weep.

"FAR, FAR AWAY."

    I touch thy temples pale !
      I breathe my soul on thee !
    And could my prayers avail,
      All my joy should be
Dead, and I would live to weep,
So thou might'st win one hour of quiet sleep.

LINES.

I.

Far, far away, O ye
Halcyons of memory,
Seek some far calmer nest
Than this abandoned breast;—
No news of your false spring
To my heart's winter bring,
Once having gone, in vain
      Ye come again.

II.

Vultures, who build your bowers
High in the Future's towers,
Withered hopes on hopes are spread,
Dying joys choked by the dead,
Will serve your beaks for prey
      Many a day.

THE FUGITIVES.

I.

The waters are flashing,
The white hail is dashing,
The lightnings are glancing,
The hoar-spray is dancing —
  Away!

The whirlwind is rolling,
The thunder is tolling,
The forest is swinging,
The minster bells ringing —
  Come away!

The Earth is like Ocean,
Wreck-strewn and in motion:
Bird, beast, man and worm
Have crept out of the storm —
  Come away!

II.

"Our boat has one sail,
And the helmsman is pale; —

THE FUGITIVES.

A bold pilot I trow,
Who should follow us now,"—
    Shouted He—

And she cried: "Ply the oar!
Put off gaily from shore!"—
As she spoke, bolts of death
Mixed with hail, specked their path
    O'er the sea.

And from isle, tower and rock,
The blue beacon cloud broke,
And though dumb in the blast,
The red cannon flashed fast
    From the lee.

III.

"And fear'st thou, and fear'st thou?
And see'st thou, and hear'st thou?
And drive we not free
O'er the terrible sea,
    I and thou?"

One boat-cloak did cover
The loved and the lover—
Their blood beats one measure,
They murmur proud pleasure
    Soft and low;—

THE FUGITIVES.

While around the lashed Ocean,
Like mountains in motion,
Is withdrawn and uplifted,
Sunk, shattered and shifted
    To and fro.

IV.

In the court of the fortress
Beside the pale portress,
Like a blood-hound well beaten,
The bridegroom stands, eaten
    By shame;

On the topmost watch-turret,
As a death-boding spirit,
Stands the grey tyrant father,
To his voice the mad weather
    Seems tame;

And with curses as wild
As e'er clung to child,
He devotes to the blast
The best, loveliest and last
    Of his name!

SONG.

I.

RARELY, rarely, comest thou,
   Spirit of Delight!
Wherefore hast thou left me now
   Many a day and night?
Many a weary night and day
'Tis since thou art fled away.

II.

How shall ever one like me
   Win thee back again?
With the joyous and the free
   Thou wilt scoff at pain.
Spirit false! thou hast forgot
All but those who need thee not.

III.

As a lizard with the shade
   Of a trembling leaf,
Thou with sorrow art dismayed;
   Even the sighs of grief
Reproach thee, that thou art not near,
And reproach thou wilt not hear.

"RARELY, RARELY COMEST THOU."

IV.

Let me set my mournful ditty
   To a merry measure,
Thou wilt never come for pity,
   Thou wilt come for pleasure.
Pity then will cut away
Those cruel wings, and thou wilt stay.

V.

I love all that thou lovest,
   Spirit of Delight!
The fresh Earth in new leaves drest,
   And the starry night;
Autumn evening, and the morn
When the golden mists are born.

VI.

I love snow, and all the forms
   Of the radiant frost;
I love waves, and winds, and storms,
   Every thing almost
Which is Nature's, and may be
Untainted by man's misery.

VII.

I love tranquil solitude,
   And such society

"MUSIC, WHEN SOFT VOICES DIE."

As is quiet, wise and good;
   Between thee and me
What difference? but thou dost possess
The things I seek, not love them less.

VIII.

I love Love — though he has wings,
   And like light can flee,
But above all other things,
   Spirit, I love thee —
Thou art love and life! O come,
Make once more my heart thy home.

TO ⸺.

Music, when soft voices die,
Vibrates in the memory —
Odours, when sweet violets sicken,
Live within the sense they quicken.
Rose leaves, when the rose is dead,
Are heaped for the belovèd's bed;
And so thy thoughts, when thou art gone,
Love itself shall slumber on.

MUTABILITY.

I.

THE flower that smiles to-day
          To-morrow dies;
All that we wish to stay
          Tempts and then flies.
What is this world's delight?
Lightning that mocks the night,
      Brief even as bright.

II.

Virtue, how frail it is!
          Friendship how rare!
Love, how it sells poor bliss
          For proud despair!
But we, though soon they fall,
Survive their joy, and all
      Which ours we call.

III.

Whilst skies are blue and bright,
          Whilst flowers are gay,
Whilst eyes that change ere night
          Make glad the day;

POLITICAL GREATNESS.

Whilst yet the calm hours creep,
Dream thou — and from thy sleep
Then wake to weep.

SONNET.

POLITICAL GREATNESS.

Nor happiness, nor majesty, nor fame,
Nor peace, nor strength, nor skill in arms or arts,
Shepherd those herds whom tyranny makes tame;
Verse echoes not one beating of their hearts,
History is but the shadow of their shame,
Art veils her glass, or from the pageant starts
As to oblivion their blind millions fleet,
Staining that Heaven with obscene imagery
Of their own likeness. What are numbers knit
By force or custom? Man who man would be,
Must rule the empire of himself; in it
Must be supreme, establishing his throne
On vanquished will, quelling the anarchy
Of hopes and fears, being himself alone.

THE AZIOLA.

I.

"Do you not hear the Aziola cry?
    Methinks she must be nigh,"
      Said Mary, as we sate
In dusk, ere stars were lit, or candles brought;
      And I, who thought
   This Aziola was some tedious woman,
     Asked, "Who is Aziola?" How elate
I felt to know that it was nothing human,
    No mockery of myself to fear or hate:
      And Mary saw my soul,
And laughed, and said, "Disquiet yourself not;
    'Tis nothing but a little downy owl."

II.

Sad Aziola! many an eventide
    Thy music I had heard
By wood and stream, meadow and mountain side,
    And fields and marshes wide,
Such as nor voice, nor lute, nor wind, nor bird,
    The soul ever stirred;
Unlike and far sweeter than them all.
Sad Aziola! from that moment I
    Loved thee and thy sad cry.

REMEMBRANCE.

I.

SWIFTER far than summer's flight —
Swifter far than youth's delight —
Swifter far than happy night,
    Art thou come and gone —
As the wood when leaves are shed,
As the night when sleep is fled,
As the heart when joy is dead,
    I am left alone, alone.

II.

The swallow summer comes again —
The owlet night resumes his reign —
But the wild-swan youth is fain
    To fly with thee, false as thou. —
My heart each day desires the morrow;
Sleep itself is turned to sorrow;
Vainly would my winter borrow
    Sunny leaves from any bough.

III.

Lilies for a bridal bed —
Roses for a matron's head —
Violets for a maiden dead —

A LAMENT.

> Pansies let *my* flowers be:
> On the living grave I bear
> Scatter them without a tear —
> Let no friend, however dear,
> > Waste one hope, one fear for me.

A LAMENT.

I.

Oh, world! oh, life! oh, time!
On whose last steps I climb
  Trembling at that where I had stood before;
When will return the glory of your prime?
  No more — O, never more!

II.

Out of the day and night
A joy has taken flight;
  Fresh spring, and summer, and winter hoar,
Move my faint heart with grief, but with delight
  No more — O, never more!

TO EDWARD WILLIAMS.

I.

The serpent is shut out from paradise.
    The wounded deer must seek the herb no more
        In which its heart-cure lies:
    The widowed dove must cease to haunt a bower
Like that from which its mate with feignèd sighs
        Fled in the April hour.
    I too must seldom seek again
Near happy friends a mitigated pain.

II.

Of hatred I am proud, — with scorn content;
    Indifference, that once hurt me, now is grown
        Itself indifferent.
    But, not to speak of love, pity alone
Can break a spirit already more than bent.
        The miserable one
    Turns the mind's poison into food, —
Its medicine is tears, — its evil good.

TO EDWARD WILLIAMS.

III.

Therefore, if now I see you seldomer,
    Dear friends, dear *friend!* know that I only fly
        Your looks, because they stir
    Griefs that should sleep, and hopes that cannot die:
The very comfort that they minister
        I scarce can bear, yet I,
    So deeply is the arrow gone,
Should quickly perish if it were withdrawn.

IV.

When I return to my cold home, you ask
    Why I am not as I have ever been.
        You spoil me for the task
    Of acting a forced part in life's dull scene,—
Of wearing on my brow the idle mask
        Of author, great or mean,
    In the world's carnival. I sought
Peace thus, and but in you I found it not.

V.

Full half an hour, to-day, I tried my lot
    With various flowers, and every one still said,
        "She loves me —— loves me not."
    And if this meant a vision long since fled —

TO EDWARD WILLIAMS.

If it meant fortune, fame, or peace of thought —
    If it meant, — but I dread
      To speak what you may know too well:
Still there was truth in the sad oracle.

VI.

The crane o'er seas and forests seeks her home;
    No bird so wild but has its quiet nest,
      When it no more would roam;
    The sleepless billows on the ocean's breast
Break like a bursting heart, and die in foam,
      And thus at length find rest.
    Doubtless there is a place of peace
Where *my* weak heart and all its throbs will cease.

VII.

I asked her, yesterday, if she believed
    That I had resolution. One who *had*
      Would ne'er have thus relieved
    His heart with words, — but what his judgment bade
Would do, and leave the scorner unrelieved.
      These verses are too sad
    To send to you, but that I know,
Happy yourself, you feel another's woe.

"ONE WORD IS TOO OFTEN PROFANED."

TO ———.

I.

One word is too often profaned
    For me to profane it,
One feeling too falsely disdained
    For thee to disdain it.
One hope is too like despair
    For prudence to smother,
And pity from thee more dear
    Than that from another.

II.

I can give not what men call love,
    But wilt thou accept not
The worship the heart lifts above
    And the Heavens reject not,
The desire of the moth for the star,
    Of the night for the morrow,
The devotion to something afar
    From the sphere of our sorrow?

TO ———.

I.

When passion's trance is overpast,
If tenderness and truth could last
Or live, whilst all wild feelings keep
Some mortal slumber, dark and deep,
I should not weep, I should not weep!

II.

It were enough to feel, to see,
Thy soft eyes gazing tenderly,
And dream the rest — and burn and be
The secret food of fires unseen,
Couldst thou but be as thou hast been.

III.

After the slumber of the year
The woodland violets re-appear,
All things revive in field or grove,
And sky and sea, but two, which move,
And form all others, life and love.

A BRIDAL SONG.

I.

The golden gates of Sleep unbar
   Where Strength and Beauty met together,
Kindle their image like a star
   In a sea of glassy weather.
Night, with all thy stars look down,—
   Darkness, weep thy holiest dew,—
Never smiled the inconstant moon
      On a pair so true.
Let eyes not see their own delight;—
Haste, swift Hour, and thy flight
      Oft renew.

II.

Fairies, sprites, and angels keep her!
   Holy stars, permit no wrong!
And return to wake the sleeper,
      Dawn,—ere it be long!
Oh joy! oh fear! what will be done
In the absence of the sun!
      Come along!

GINEVRA.

Wild, pale, and wonder-stricken, even as one
Who staggers forth into the air and sun
From the dark chamber of a mortal fever,
Bewildered, and incapable, and ever
Fancying strange comments in her dizzy brain
Of usual shapes, till the familiar train
Of objects and of persons past like things
Strange as a dreamer's mad imaginings,
Ginevra from the nuptial altar went;
The vows to which her lips had sworn assent
Rung in her brain still with a jarring din,
Deafening the lost intelligence within.

And so she moved under the bridal veil,
Which made the paleness of her cheek more pale,
And deepened the faint crimson of her mouth,
And darkened her dark locks, as moonlight doth, —
And of the gold and jewels glittering there
She scarce felt conscious, — but the weary glare
Lay like a chaos of unwelcome light,
Vexing the sense with gorgeous undelight.

GINEVRA.

A moonbeam in the shadow of a cloud
Was less heavenly fair — her face was bowed,
And as she past, the diamonds in her hair
Were mirrored in the polished marble stair
Which led from the cathedral to the street;
And ever as she went her light fair feet
Erased these images.

   The bride-maidens who round her thronging can
Some with a sense of self-rebuke and shame,
Envying the unenviable; and others
Making the joy which should have been another's
Their own by gentle sympathy; and some
Sighing to think of an unhappy home:
Some few admiring what can ever lure
Maidens to leave the heaven serene and pure
Of parents' smiles for life's great cheat; a thing
Bitter to taste, sweet in imagining.

   But they are all dispersed — and, lo! she stands
Looking in idle grief on her white hands,
Alone within the garden now her own;
And through the sunny air, with jangling tone,
The music of the merry marriage bells,
Killing the azure silence, sinks and swells;—
Absorbed like one within a dream who dreams
That he is dreaming, until slumber seems

GINEVRA.

A mockery of itself — when suddenly
Antonio stood before her, pale as she.
With agony, with sorrow, and with pride,
He lifted his wan eyes upon the bride,
And said — " Is this thy faith?" and then as one
Whose sleeping face is stricken by the sun
With light like a harsh voice, which bids him rise
And look upon his day of life with eyes
Which weep in vain that they can dream no more,
Ginevra saw her lover, and forbore
To shriek or faint, and checked the stifling blood
Rushing upon her heart, and unsubdued
Said — " Friend, if earthly violence or ill,
Suspicion, doubt, or the tyrannic will
Of parents, chance, or custom, time or change,
Or circumstance, or terror, or revenge,
Or wildered looks, or words, or evil speech,
With all their stings and venom can impeach
Our love, — we love not : — if the grave which hides
The victim from the tyrant, and divides
The cheek that whitens from the eyes that dart
Imperious inquisition to the heart
That is another's, could dissever ours,
We love not." — "What ! do not the silent hours
Beckon thee to Gherardi's bridal bed?
Is not that ring " —— a pledge, he would have said,

Of broken vows, but she with patient look
The golden circle from her finger took,
And said — "Accept this token of my faith,
The pledge of vows to be absolved by death;
And I am dead or shall be soon — my knell
Will mix it's music with that merry bell,
Does it not sound as if they sweetly said
'We toll a corpse out of the marriage bed?'
The flowers upon my bridal chamber strewn,
Will serve unfaded for my bier — so soon
That even the dying violet will not die
Before Ginevra." The strong fantasy
Had made her accents weaker and more weak,
And quenched the crimson life upon her cheek,
And glazed her eyes, and spread an atmosphere
Round her, which chilled the burning noon with fear
Making her but an image of the thought,
Which, like a prophet or a shadow, brought
News of the terrors of the coming time.
Like an accuser branded with the crime
He would have cast on a belovèd friend,
Whose dying eyes reproach not to the end
The pale betrayer — he then with vain repentance
Would share, he cannot now avert, the sentence —
Antonio stood and would have spoken, when
The compound voice of women and of men

Was heard approaching; he retired, while she
Was led amid the admiring company
Back to the palace, — and her maidens soon
Changed her attire for the afternoon,
And left her at her own request to keep
An hour of quiet and rest: — like one asleep
With open eyes and folded hands she lay,
Pale in the light of the declining day.

  Meanwhile the day sinks fast, the sun is set,
And in the lighted hall the guests are met;
The beautiful looked lovelier in the light
Of love, and admiration, and delight
Reflected from a thousand hearts and eyes
Kindling a momentary Paradise.
This crowd is safer than the silent wood,
Where love's own doubts disturb the solitude;
On frozen hearts the fiery rain of wine
Falls, and the dew of music more divine
Tempers the deep emotions of the time
To spirits cradled in a sunny clime: —
How many meet, who never yet have met,
To part too soon, but never to forget.
How many saw the beauty, power and wit
Of looks and words which ne'er inchanted yet;
But life's familiar veil was now withdrawn,
As the world leaps before an earthquake's dawn,

And unprophetic of the coming hours,
The matin winds from the expanded flowers,
Scatter their hoarded incense, and awaken
The earth, until the dewy sleep is shaken
From every living heart which it possesses,
Through seas and winds, cities and wildernesses,
As if the future and the past were all
Treasured i' the instant;—so Gherardi's hall
Laughed in the mirth of its lord's festival,
Till some one asked—"Where is the Bride?" And then
A bride's-maid went,—and ere she came again
A silence fell upon the guests—a pause
Of expectation, as when beauty awes
All hearts with its approach, though unbeheld;
Then wonder, and then fear that wonder quelled;—
For whispers past from mouth to ear which drew
The colour from the hearer's cheeks, and flew
Louder and swifter round the company;
And then Gherardi entered with an eye
Of ostentatious trouble, and a crowd
Surrounded him, and some were weeping loud.

They found Ginevra dead! if it be death,
To lie without motion, or pulse, or breath,
With waxen cheeks, and limbs cold, stiff, and white,
And open eyes, whose fixed and glassy light

Mocked at the speculation they had owned.
If it be death, when there is felt around
A smell of clay, a pale and icy glare,
And silence, and a sense that lifts the hair
From the scalp to the ancles, as it were
Corruption from the spirit passing forth,
And giving all it shrouded to the earth,
And leaving as swift lightning in its flight
Ashes, and smoke, and darkness: in our night
Of thought we know thus much of death, — no more
Than the unborn dream of our life before
Their barks are wrecked on its inhospitable shore.
The marriage feast and its solemnity
Was turned to funeral pomp — the company
With heavy hearts and looks, broke up; nor they
Who loved the dead went weeping on their way
Alone, but sorrow mixed with sad surprise
Loosened the springs of pity in all eyes,
On which that form, whose fate they weep in vain,
Will never, thought they, kindle smiles again.
The lamps which half extinguished in their haste
Gleamed few and faint o'er the abandoned feast,
Showed as it were within the vaulted room
A cloud of sorrow hanging, as if gloom
Had past out of men's minds into the air.
Some few yet stood around Gherardi there,

GINEVRA.

Friends and relations of the dead, — and he,
A loveless man, accepted torpidly
The consolation that he wanted not,
Awe in the place of grief within him wrought.
Their whispers made the solemn silence seem
More still — some wept, . . .
Some melted into tears without a sob,
And some with hearts that might be heard to throb
Leant on the table, and at intervals
Shuddered to hear through the deserted halls
And corridors the thrilling shrieks which came
Upon the breeze of night, that shook the flame
Of every torch and taper as it swept
From out the chamber where the women kept; —
Their tears fell on the dear companion cold
Of pleasures now departed; then was knolled
The bell of death, and soon the priests arrived,
And finding death their penitent had shrived,
Returned like ravens from a corpse whereon
A vulture has just feasted to the bone.
And then the mourning women came. —

* * * * *

THE DIRGE.

Old winter was gone
In his weakness back to the mountains hoar,
And the spring came down

GINEVRA.

From the planet that hovers upon the shore
   Where the sea of sunlight encroaches
On the limits of wintry night;—
If the land, and the air, and the sea
   Rejoice not when spring approaches,
We did not rejoice in thee,
        Ginevra!

She is still, she is cold
        On the bridal couch,
One step to the white death-bed,
        And one to the bier,
And one to the charnel — and one, O where?
        The dark arrow fled
        In the noon.

Ere the sun through heaven once more has rolled,
The rats in her heart
Will have made their nest,
And the worms be alive in her golden hair,
While the spirit that guides the sun,
Sits throned in his flaming chair,
        She shall sleep.

EVENING.

PONTE A MARE, PISA.

I.

The sun is set; the swallows are asleep;
  The bats are flitting fast in the grey air;
The slow soft toads out of damp corners creep,
  And evening's breath, wandering here and there
Over the quivering surface of the stream,
Wakes not one ripple from its summer dream.

II.

There is no dew on the dry grass to-night,
  Nor damp within the shadow of the trees;
The wind is intermitting, dry, and light;
  And in the inconstant motion of the breeze
The dust and straws are driven up and down,
And whirled about the pavement of the town.

III.

Within the surface of the fleeting river
  The wrinkled image of the city lay,
Immovably unquiet, and for ever
  It trembles, but it never fades away;
Go to the . . .
You, being changed, will find it then as now.

IV.

The chasm in which the sun has sunk is shut
   By darkest barriers of cinereous cloud,
Like mountain over mountain huddled — but
   Growing and moving upwards in a crowd,
And over it a space of watery blue,
Which the keen evening star is shining through.

TO-MORROW.

I.

WHERE art thou, beloved To-morrow?
   When young and old and strong and weak,
Rich and poor, through joy and sorrow,
   Thy sweet smiles we ever seek, —
In thy place — ah! well-a-day!
We find the thing we fled — To-day.

II.

If I walk in Autumn's even
   While the dead leaves pass,
If I look on Spring's soft heaven, —
   Something is not there which was.
Winter's wondrous frost and snow,
Summer's clouds, where are they now?

MUSIC.

I.

I PANT for the music which is divine,
   My heart in its thirst is a dying flower;
Pour forth the sound like inchanted wine,
   Loosen the notes in a silver shower;
Like a herbless plain, for the gentle rain,
I gasp, I faint, till they wake again.

II.

Let me drink of the spirit of that sweet sound,
   More, O more,—I am thirsting yet,
It loosens the serpent which care has bound
   Upon my heart to stifle it;
The dissolving strain, through every vein,
Passes into my heart and brain.

III.

As the scent of a violet withered up,
   Which grew by the brink of a silver lake;
When the hot noon has drained its dewy cup,
   And mist there was none its thirst to slake—
And the violet lay dead while the odour flew
On the wings of the wind o'er the waters blue—

IV.

As one who drinks from a charmèd cup
   Of foaming, and sparkling and murmuring wine,
Whom, a mighty Enchantress filling up,
   Invites to love with her kiss divine. . . .

THE ZUCCA.

I.

Summer was dead and Autumn was expiring,
   And infant Winter laughed upon the land
All cloudlessly and cold;—when I, desiring
   More in this world than any understand,
Wept o'er the beauty, which like sea retiring,
   Had left the earth bare as the wave-worn sand
Of my lorn heart, and o'er the grass and flowers
Pale for the falsehood of the flattering Hours.

II.

Summer was dead, but I yet lived to weep
   The instability of all but weeping;
And on the Earth lulled in her winter sleep
   I woke, and envied her as she was sleeping.

Too happy Earth! over thy face shall creep
　The wakening vernal airs, until thou, leaping
From unremembered dreams, shalt　　　see
No death divide thy immortality.

III.

I loved — O no, I mean not one of ye,
　Or any earthly one, though ye are dear
As human heart to human heart may be; —
　I loved, I know not what — but this low sphere
And all that it contains, contains not thee,
　Thou, whom seen nowhere, I feel everywhere.
From heaven and earth, and all that in them are,
Veiled art thou, like a　　　　　star.

IV.

By Heaven and Earth, from all whose shapes flowest,
　Neither to be contained, delayed, nor hidden,
Making divine the loftiest and the lowest,
　When for a moment thou art not forbidden
To live within the life which thou bestowest;
　And leaving noblest things vacant and chidden,
Cold as a corpse after the spirit's flight,
Blank as the sun after the birth of night.

V.

In winds, and trees, and streams, and all things common.
   In music and the sweet unconscious tone
Of animals, and voices which are human,
   Meant to express some feelings of their own;
In the soft motions and rare smile of woman,
   In flowers and leaves, and in the grass fresh-shewn,
Or dying in the autumn, I the most
Adore thee present or lament thee lost.

VI.

And thus I went lamenting, when I saw
   A plant upon the river's margin lie,
Like one who loved beyond his Nature's law,
   And in despair had cast him down to die;
Its leaves which had outlived the frost, the thaw
   Had blighted; like a heart which hatred's eye
Can blast not, but which pity kills; the dew
Lay on its spotted leaves like tears too true.

VII.

The Heavens had wept upon it, but the Earth
   Had crushed it on her unmaternal breast.

    *   *   *   *   *

VIII.

I bore it to my chamber, and I planted
  It in a vase full of the lightest mould;
The winter beams which out of Heaven slanted
  Fell through the window panes, disrobed of cold,
Upon its leaves and flowers; the star which panted
  In evening for the Day, whose car has rolled
Over the horizon's wave, with looks of light
Smiled on it from the threshold of the night.

IX.

The mitigated influences of air
  And light revived the plant, and from it grew
Strong leaves and tendrils, and its flowers fair,
  Full as a cup with the vine's burning dew,
O'erflowed with golden colours; an atmosphere
  Of vital warmth infolded it anew,
And every impulse sent to every part
The unbeheld pulsations of its heart.

X.

Well might the plant grow beautiful and strong,
  Even if the air and sun had smiled not on it;
For one wept o'er it all the winter long
  Tears pure as Heaven's rain, which fell upon it

A DIRGE.

Hour after hour; for sounds of softest song
  Mixed with the stringèd melodies that won it
To leave the gentle lips on which it slept,
Had loosed the heart of him who sat and wept.

XI.

Had loosed his heart, and shook the leaves and flowers
  On which he wept, the while the savage storm
Waked by the darkest of December's hours
  Was raving round the chamber hushed and warm;
The birds were shivering in their leafless bowers,
  The fish were frozen in the pools, the form
Of every summer plant was dead . . .
Whilst this . . .

    *   *   *   *   *

A DIRGE.

Rough wind, that moanest loud
  Grief too sad for song;
Wild wind, when sullen cloud
  Knells all the night long;
Sad storm, whose tears are vain,
Bare woods, whose branches stain,
Deep caves and dreary main,
  Wail, for the world's wrong!

THE MAGNETIC LADY TO HER PATIENT

I.

"Sleep, sleep on! forget thy pain;
  My hand is on thy brow,
My spirit on thy brain;
My pity on thy heart, poor friend;
  And from my fingers flow
The powers of life, and like a sign,
  Seal thee from thine hour of woe;
And brood on thee, but may not blend
    With thine.

II.

"Sleep, sleep on! I love thee not;
  But when I think that he
Who made and makes my lot
As full of flowers as thine of weeds,
  Might have been lost like thee;
And that a hand which was not mine,
  Might then have charmed his agony
As I another's — my heart bleeds
    For thine.

III.

"Sleep, sleep, and with the slumber of
  The dead and the unborn
Forget thy life and love;
Forget that thou must wake for ever;
  Forget the world's dull scorn;
Forget lost health, and the divine
  Feelings which died in youth's brief morn;
And forget me, for I can never
    Be thine.

IV.

" Like a cloud big with a May shower,
  My soul weeps healing rain,
On thee, thou withered flower;
It breathes mute music on thy sleep;
  Its odour calms thy brain;
Its light within thy gloomy breast
  Spreads like a second youth again.
By mine thy being is to its deep
    Possest.

V.

"The spell is done. How feel you now?"
  "Better — Quite well," replied

"WHEN THE LAMP IS SHATTERED."

The sleeper. — "What would do
You good when suffering and awake?
What cure your head and side? — "
"What would cure, that would kill me, Jane:
And as I must on earth abide
Awhile, yet tempt me not to break
My chain."

LINES.

I.

When the lamp is shattered
The light in the dust lies dead —
When the cloud is scattered
The rainbow's glory is shed.
When the lute is broken,
Sweet tones are remembered not;
When the lips have spoken,
Loved accents are soon forgot.

II.

As music and splendour
Survive not the lamp and the lute,

"WHEN THE LAMP IS SHATTERED."

The heart's echoes render
No song when the spirit is mute:—
  No song but sad dirges,
Like the wind through a ruined cell,
  Or the mournful surges
That ring the dead seaman's knell.

III.

When hearts have once mingled
Love first leaves the well-built nest,
  The weak one is singled
To endure what it once possest.
  O, Love! who bewailest
The frailty of all things here,
  Why choose you the frailest
For your cradle, your home and your bier?

IV.

Its passions will rock thee
As the storms rock the ravens on high:
  Bright reason will mock thee,
Like the sun from a wintry sky.
  From thy nest every rafter
Will rot, and thine eagle home
  Leave thee naked to laughter,
When leaves fall and cold winds come.

TO JANE—THE INVITATION.

Best and brightest, come away!
Fairer far than this fair Day,
Which, like thee to those in sorrow,
Comes to bid a sweet good-morrow
To the rough Year just awake
In its cradle on the brake.
The brightest hour of unborn Spring,
Through the winter wandering,
Found, it seems, the halcyon Morn
To hoar February born;
Bending from Heaven, in azure mirth,
It kissed the forehead of the Earth,
And smiled upon the silent sea,
And bade the frozen streams be free,
And waked to music all their fountains,
And breathed upon the frozen mountains,
And like a prophetess of May
Strewed flowers upon the barren way,
Making the wintry world appear
Like one on whom thou smilest, dear.

TO JANE — THE INVITATION.

Away, away, from men and towns,
To the wild wood and the downs —
To the silent wilderness
Where the soul need not repress
Its music lest it should not find
An echo in another's mind,
While the touch of Nature's art
Harmonizes heart to heart.
I leave this notice on my door
For each accustomed visitor: —
"I am gone into the fields
To take what this sweet hour yields; —
Reflection, you may come to-morrow,
Sit by the fireside with Sorrow. —
You with the unpaid bill, Despair, —
You tiresome verse-reciter, Care, —
I will pay you in the grave, —
Death will listen to your stave.
Expectation too, be off!
To-day is for itself enough;
Hope in pity mock not Woe
With smiles, nor follow where I go;
Long having lived on thy sweet food,
At length I find one moment's good
After long pain — with all your love,
This you never told me of."

TO JANE — THE INVITATION.

Radiant sister of the Day,
Awake! arise! and come away!
To the wild woods and the plains,
And the pools where winter rains
Image all their roof of leaves,
Where the pine its garland weaves
Of sapless green and ivy dun
Round stems that never kiss the sun;
Where the lawns and pastures be,
And the sandhills of the sea;—
Where the melting hoar-frost wets
The daisy-star that never sets,
And wind-flowers, and violets,
Which yet join not scent to hue,
Crown the pale year weak and new;
When the night is left behind
In the deep east, dun and blind,
And the blue noon is over us,
And the multitudinous
Billows murmur at our feet,
Where the earth and ocean meet,
And all things seem only one
In the universal sun.

TO JANE—THE RECOLLECTION.

I.

Now the last day of many days,
   All beautiful and bright as thou,
     The loveliest and the last, is dead,
Rise, Memory, and write its praise!
Up to thy wonted work! come, trace
     The epitaph of glory fled,—
For now the Earth has changed its face,
   A frown is on the Heaven's brow.

II.

We wandered to the Pine Forest
    That skirts the Ocean's foam,
The lightest wind was in its nest,
    The tempest in its home.
The whispering waves were half asleep,
    The clouds were gone to play,
And on the bosom of the deep,
    The smile of Heaven lay;
It seemed as if the hour were one
    Sent from beyond the skies,
Which scattered from above the sun
    A light of Paradise.

TO JANE — THE RECOLLECTION.

III.

We paused amid the pines that stood
  The giants of the waste,
Tortured by storms to shapes as rude
  As serpents interlaced,
And soothed by every azure breath,
  That under heaven is blown,
To harmonies and hues beneath,
  As tender as its own;
Now all the tree-tops lay asleep,
  Like green waves on the sea,
As still as in the silent deep
  The ocean woods may be.

IV.

How calm it was! — the silence there
  By such a chain was bound
That even the busy woodpecker
  Made stiller by her sound
The inviolable quietness;
  The breath of peace we drew
With its soft motion made not less
  The calm that round us grew.
There seemed from the remotest seat
  Of the white mountain waste,

TO JANE — THE RECOLLECTION.

To the soft flower beneath our feet,
 A magic circle traced, —
A spirit interfused around,
 A thrilling silent life,
To momentary peace it bound
 Our mortal nature's strife ; —
And still I felt the centre of
 The magic circle there,
Was one fair form that filled with love
 The lifeless atmosphere.

    v.

We paused beside the pools that lie
 Under the forest bough,
Each seemed as 'twere a little sky
 Gulphed in a world below ;
A firmament of purple light,
 Which in the dark earth lay,
More boundless than the depth of night,
 And purer than the day —
In which the lovely forests grew
 As in the upper air,
More perfect both in shape and hue
 Than any spreading there.
There lay the glade and neighbouring lawn,
 And through the dark green wood

TO JANE — THE RECOLLECTION.

The white sun twinkling like the dawn
    Out of a speckled cloud.
Sweet views which in our world above
    Can never well be seen,
Were imaged by the water's love
    Of that fair forest green.
And all was interfused beneath
    With an elysian glow,
An atmosphere without a breath,
    A softer day below.
Like one beloved the scene had lent
    To the dark water's breast,
Its every leaf and lineament
    With more than truth exprest;
Until an envious wind crept by,
    Like an unwelcome thought,
Which from the mind's too faithful eye
    Blots one dear image out.
Though thou art ever fair and kind,
    The forest ever green,
Less oft is peace in Shelley's mind,
    Than calm in waters seen.

WITH A GUITAR, TO JANE.

ARIEL to Miranda. — Take
This slave of Music, for the sake
Of him who is the slave of thee,
And teach it all the harmony
In which thou canst, and only thou,
Make the delighted spirit glow,
Till joy denies itself again,
And, too intense, is turned to pain;
For by commission and command
Of thine own Prince Ferdinand,
Poor Ariel sends this silent token
Of more than ever can be spoken;
Your guardian spirit, Ariel, who,
From life to life, must still pursue
Your happiness; — for thus alone
Can Ariel ever find his own.
From Prospero's inchanted cell,
As the mighty verses tell,
To the throne of Naples, he
Lit you o'er the trackless sea,

WITH A GUITAR, TO JANE.

Flitting on, your prow before,
Like a living meteor.
When you die, the silent Moon,
In her interlunar swoon,
Is not sadder in her cell
Than deserted Ariel.
When you live again on earth,
Like an unseen star of birth,
Ariel guides you o'er the sea
Of life from your nativity.
Many changes have been run,
Since Ferdinand and you begun
Your course of love, and Ariel still
Has tracked your steps, and served your will;
Now, in humbler, happier lot,
This is all remembered not;
And now, alas! the poor sprite is
Imprisoned, for some fault of his,
In a body like a grave;—
From you he only dares to crave,
For his service and his sorrow,
A smile to-day, a song to-morrow.

The artist who this idol wrought,
To echo all harmonious thought,
Felled a tree, while on the steep
The woods were in their winter sleep,

Rocked in that repose divine
On the wind-swept Apennine;
And dreaming, some of Autumn past,
And some of Spring approaching fast,
And some of April buds and showers,
And some of songs in July bowers,
And all of love; and so this tree,—
O that such our death may be!—
Died in sleep, and felt no pain,
To live in happier form again:
From which, beneath Heaven's fairest star,
The artist wrought this loved Guitar,
And taught it justly to reply,
To all who question skilfully,
In language gentle as thine own;
Whispering in enamoured tone
Sweet oracles of woods and dells,
And summer winds in sylvan cells;
For it had learnt all harmonies
Of the plains and of the skies,
Of the forests and the mountains,
And the many-voicèd fountains;
The clearest echoes of the hills,
The softest notes of falling rills,
The melodies of birds and bees,
The murmuring of summer seas,

And pattering rain, and breathing dew,
And airs of evening; and it knew
That seldom-heard mysterious sound,
Which, driven on its diurnal round,
As it floats through boundless day,
Our world enkindles on its way —
All this it knows, but will not tell
To those who cannot question well
The spirit that inhabits it;
It talks according to the wit
Of its companions; and no more
Is heard than has been felt before,
By those who tempt it to betray
These secrets of an elder day:
But sweetly as its answers will
Flatter hands of perfect skill,
It keeps its highest, holiest tone
For our belovèd Jane alone.

TO JANE.

I.

The keen stars were twinkling,
And the fair moon was rising among them,
  Dear Jane!

TO JANE.

The guitar was tinkling,
But the notes were not sweet till you sung them
    Again.

II.

As the moon's soft splendour
O'er the faint cold starlight of heaven
    Is thrown,
So your voice most tender
To the strings without soul had then given
    Its own.

III.

The stars will awaken,
Though the moon sleep a full hour later,
    To-night;
No leaf will be shaken
Whilst the dews of your melody scatter
    Delight.

IV.

Though the sound overpowers,
Sing again, with your dear voice revealing
    A tone
Of some world far from ours,
Where music and moonlight and feeling
    Are one.

LINES WRITTEN IN THE BAY OF LERICI.

She left me at the silent time
When the moon had ceased to climb
The azure path of Heaven's steep,
And like an albatross asleep,
Balanced on her wings of light,
Hovered in the purple night,
Ere she sought her ocean nest
In the chambers of the West.
She left me, and I staid alone
Thinking over every tone
Which, though silent to the ear,
The inchanted heart could hear,
Like notes which die when born, but still
Haunt the echoes of the hill;
And feeling ever — O too much ! —
The soft vibration of her touch,
As if her gentle hand, even now,
Lightly trembled on my brow;
And thus, although she absent were,
Memory gave me all of her

That even Fancy dares to claim: —
Her presence had made weak and tame
All passions, and I lived alone
In the time which is our own;
The past and future were forgot,
As they had been, and would be, not.
But soon, the guardian angel gone,
The dæmon reassumed his throne
In my faint heart. I dare not speak
My thoughts, but thus disturbed and weak
I sat and saw the vessels glide
Over the ocean bright and wide,
Like spirit-wingèd chariots sent
O'er some serenest element
For ministrations strange and far;
As if to some Elysian star
Sailed for drink to medicine
Such sweet and bitter pain as mine.
And the wind that winged their flight
From the land came fresh and light,
And the scent of wingèd flowers,
And the coolness of the hours
Of dew, and sweet warmth left by day,
Were scattered o'er the twinkling bay.
And the fisher with his lamp
And spear about the low rocks damp

"WE MEET NOT AS WE PARTED."

Crept, and struck the fish which came
To worship the delusive flame.
Too happy they, whose pleasure sought
Extinguishes all sense and thought
Of the regret that pleasure leaves,
Destroying life alone, not peace!

LINES.

I.

We meet not as we parted,
   We feel more than all may see,
My bosom is heavy-hearted,
   And thine full of doubt for me.
   One moment has bound the free.

II.

That moment is gone for ever,
   Like lightning that flashed and died,
Like a snowflake upon the river,
   Like a sunbeam upon the tide,
   Which the dark shadows hide.

"WE MEET NOT AS WE PARTED."

III.

That moment from time was singled
   As the first of a life of pain,
The cup of its joy was mingled
   —Delusion too sweet though vain !
   Too sweet to be mine again.

IV.

Sweet lips, could my heart have hidden
   That its life was crushed by you,
Ye would not have then forbidden
   The death which a heart so true
   Sought in your briny dew.

V.

*   *   *   *
  *   *   *   *
*   *   *   *

Methinks too little cost
For a moment so found, so lost !

THE ISLE.

There was a little lawny islet
By anemone and violet,
    Like mosaic, paven:
And its roof was flowers and leaves
Which the summer's breath enweaves,
Where nor sun nor showers nor breeze
Pierce the pines and tallest trees,
    Each a gem engraven.
Girt by many an azure wave
With which the clouds and mountains pave
    A lake's blue chasm.

INDEX OF FIRST LINES.

	PAGE
A GLORIOUS people vibrated again	189
Alas! good friend, what profit can you see	303
And like a dying lady, lean and pale	272
A pale dream came to a Lady fair	82
A portal as of shadowy adamant	300
Arethusa arose	274
Ariel to Miranda. — Take	381
Arise, arise, arise!	158
Art thou pale for weariness	272
A Sensitive Plant in a garden grew	166
Away! the moor is dark beneath the moon	32
Before those cruel Twins, whom at one birth	241
Best and brightest, come away!	374
Camelions feed on light and air	152
Come, be happy! — sit by me	145
Death is here and death is there	226
"Do you not hear the Aziola cry?"	344
Earth, ocean, air, belovèd brotherhood!	1
Far, far away, O ye	335
From the forests and highlands	283
Good night? ah! no; the hour is ill	280
Hail to thee, blithe spirit!	184
"Here lieth One whose name was writ on water"	303

INDEX OF FIRST LINES.

	PAGE
Her voice did quiver as we parted	75
Honey from silkworms who can gather	98
How wonderful is Death	39
I arise from dreams of thee	160
I bring fresh showers for the thirsting flowers	180
I dreamed that, as I wandered by the way	278
I fear thy kisses, gentle maiden	287
I loved — alas! our life is love	149
I met a traveller from an antique land	93
I pant for the music which is divine	364
I rode one evening with Count Maddalo	116
I stood within the city disinterred	290
It lieth, gazing on the midnight sky	163
It was a bright and cheerful afternoon	289
I weep for Adonais — he is dead!	304
Lift not the painted veil which those who live	100
Like the ghost of a dear friend dead	301
Listen, listen, Mary mine	145
Madonna, wherefore hast thou sent to me	333
Many a green isle needs must be	101
Mine eyes were dim with tears unshed	65
Music, when soft voices die	341
My lost William, thou in whom	165
Nor happiness, nor majesty, nor fame	343
Now the last day of many days	377
Oh, world! oh, life! oh, time!	346
O Mary dear, that you were here	99
One word is too often profaned	350
Orphan hours, the year is dead	330
O! there are spirits of the air	30
O thou, who plumed with strong desire	285
O wild West Wind, thou breath of Autumn's being	154
Palace-roof of cloudless nights!	150
Poet of Nature, thou hast wept to know	38

INDEX OF FIRST LINES.

	PAGE
Rarely, rarely, comest thou	339
Rough wind, that moanest loud	369
Sacred Goddess, Mother Earth	288
She left me at the silent time	386
Sleep, sleep on! forget thy pain	370
Summer was dead, and autumn was expiring	365
Sweet Spirit! Sister of that orphan one	202
Swifter far than summer's flight	345
Swiftly walk over the western wave	331
Tell me, thou star, whose wings of light	299
That time is dead for ever, child	94
The awful shadow of some unseen Power	76
The billows on the beach are leaping around it	96
The cold earth slept below	67
The everlasting universe of things	65
The fiery mountains answer each other	297
The flower that smiles to-day	342
The fountains mingle with the river	273
The golden gates of Sleep unbar	352
The keen stars were twinkling	384
The odour from the flower is gone	141
The pale, the cold, and the moony smile	35
There late was One within whose subtle being	80
There was a little lawny islet	390
The rose that drinks the fountain dew	92
The serpent is shut out from paradise	347
The sleepless Hours who watch me as I lie	281
The spider spreads her webs, whether she be	228
The sun is set; the swallows are asleep	362
The sun is warm, the sky is clear	142
The warm sun is failing, the bleak wind is wailing	227
The waters are flashing	336
The wind has swept from the wide atmosphere	36
They die — the dead return not — Misery	95

INDEX OF FIRST LINES.

	PAGE
Thou art fair, and few are fairer	161
Thus to be lost and thus to sink and die	90
Unfathomable Sea! whose waves are years	333
We are as clouds that veil the midnight moon	34
We meet not as we parted	388
We strew these opiate flowers	334
What! alive and so bold, oh earth?	328
When passion's trance is overpast	351
When the lamp is shattered	372
Where art thou, beloved To-morrow?	363
Wild, pale, and wonder-stricken, even as one	353
Wilt thou forget the happy hours	144
Ye hasten to the dead! What seek ye there	302
Yet look on me — take not thine eyes away	68

CHISWICK PRESS:—C. WHITTINGHAM, TOOKS COURT, CHANCERY LANE.

PR   Shelley, Percy Bysshe
5403   Poems
G3

PLEASE DO NOT REMOVE
CARDS OR SLIPS FROM THIS POCKET

UNIVERSITY OF TORONTO LIBRARY